First World War
and Army of Occupation
War Diary
France, Belgium and Germany

3 CAVALRY DIVISION
6 Cavalry Brigade
1st/1st North Somerset Yeomanry
2 November 1914 - 31 March 1918

WO95/1153/4

The Naval & Military Press Ltd
www.nmarchive.com

Published in association with The National Archives

Published by

The Naval & Military Press Ltd

Unit 10 Ridgewood Industrial Park,

Uckfield, East Sussex,

TN22 5QE England

Tel: +44 (0) 1825 749494

www.naval-military-press.com

www.nmarchive.com

This diary has been reprinted in facsimile from the original. Any imperfections are inevitably reproduced and the quality may fall short of modern type and cartographic standards.

© Crown Copyright
Images reproduced by permission of The National Archives, London, England, 2015.

Contents

Document type	Place/Title	Date From	Date To
Heading	WO95/1153/4 3 Cavalry Division 6 Cavalry Brigade 1/1 North Somerset 4 Company Nov 1914-Mar, 1918 WO95/1153		
Heading	1914-1918 3rd Cavalry Division 6th Cavalry Brigade North Somerset Yeomanry Nov 1914-Mar 1918		
Heading	North Somerset Yeomanry November to December 1914 Vol 1 Mar 1918		
War Diary	Forest Row	02/11/1914	02/11/1914
War Diary	At Sea	03/11/1914	03/11/1914
War Diary	La Heve	04/11/1914	05/11/1914
War Diary	On Rail	06/11/1914	06/11/1914
War Diary	St Omer	07/11/1914	07/11/1914
War Diary	Esquerdes	08/11/1914	11/11/1914
War Diary	St Sylvestre	12/11/1914	12/11/1914
War Diary	Dranoutre	13/11/1914	13/11/1914
War Diary	Ypres	14/11/1914	14/11/1914
War Diary	Vlamertinghe	15/11/1914	15/11/1914
War Diary	Zillebeke	16/11/1914	17/11/1914
War Diary	Vlamertinghe	18/11/1914	20/11/1914
War Diary	Merville	21/11/1914	14/12/1914
War Diary	Bailleul	15/12/1914	16/12/1914
War Diary	Merville	17/12/1914	31/12/1914
Heading	6th Cavalry Brigade North Somerset Yeomanry Vol II 1st Jan. 28.2.15 Appendix I		
War Diary	Merville	01/01/1915	28/01/1915
War Diary	Steenbecque	29/01/1915	03/02/1915
War Diary	Ypres	04/02/1915	08/02/1915
War Diary	Trenches	09/02/1915	13/02/1915
War Diary	Ypres Steenbecque	14/02/1915	14/02/1915
War Diary	Steenbecque	15/02/1915	28/02/1915
Miscellaneous	Appendix I Transport		
Miscellaneous	Appendix II Equipment		
Miscellaneous	Appendix III Billets		
Miscellaneous	Appendix III		
Miscellaneous	Appendix IV		
Heading	6th Cavalry Brigade North Somerset Yeomanry Vol II 1-31.3.15		
War Diary	Steenbecque	01/03/1915	10/03/1915
War Diary	Merville	11/03/1915	13/03/1915
War Diary	Steenbecque	14/03/1915	31/03/1915
Heading	3rd Cavalry Division Units Somerset Yeomanry Vol III July 1-31-7-15		
War Diary	Steenbecque	01/04/1915	22/04/1915
War Diary	On The March	23/04/1915	26/04/1915
War Diary	Vlamertinghe And	27/04/1915	28/04/1915
War Diary	On The March	29/04/1915	04/05/1915
War Diary	Proven	05/05/1915	08/05/1915
War Diary	Proven Area	07/05/1915	08/05/1915
War Diary	Ypres	09/05/1915	14/05/1915
War Diary	Vlamertinghe	15/05/1915	22/05/1915

War Diary	Steenbecque	23/05/1915	28/05/1915
War Diary	Vlamertinghe Ypres	29/05/1915	06/06/1915
War Diary	Steenbecque	07/06/1915	31/07/1915
Heading	3rd Cavalry Division Units Somerset Yeo. Vol IV August 15		
War Diary	Steenbecque	01/08/1915	05/08/1915
War Diary	Estree Blanche	06/08/1915	01/09/1915
Miscellaneous	Sept 19, 1915 North Somerset Yeomanry		
Miscellaneous	App. III Billets		
Miscellaneous	Weekly Return of Casualties. App. V		
Heading	6 Cav. Bde. 3rd Cav. Div.The North Somerset Yeomanry September 1915		
War Diary	Estree Blanche	01/09/1915	20/09/1915
War Diary	Bois De Dames	21/09/1915	25/09/1915
War Diary	Vermelles Stn.	26/09/1915	26/09/1915
War Diary	Loos	26/09/1915	28/09/1915
War Diary	Bois De Dames	29/09/1915	30/09/1915
Miscellaneous	Appendix IV		
Miscellaneous	Strength App IV		
Heading	8th Cavalry Bde Nth Somerset Yeo Oct. 1915 Vol VI		
War Diary	Bois De Dames	01/10/1915	02/10/1915
War Diary	Bois De Dames Ferfay	03/10/1915	03/10/1915
War Diary	Ferfay	04/10/1915	18/10/1915
War Diary	Laires	19/10/1915	20/10/1915
War Diary	Amettes	21/10/1915	31/10/1915
Heading	3rd Cavalry Division Nth Somerset Yeo Nov. 1915 Vol. VII		
War Diary	Amettes	01/11/1915	16/11/1915
War Diary	On The March	17/11/1915	17/11/1915
War Diary	Hesmond	18/11/1915	30/11/1915
Heading	3rd Cav Div Nth Somerset Yeo Dec 1915 Vol VIII		
War Diary	Hesmond	01/12/1915	26/12/1915
Heading	3rd Cav North Somerset Yeo Jan. 1916 Vol IX		
War Diary	Hesmond	01/01/1916	30/04/1916
War Diary	Hesmond Paris-Plage	01/05/1916	01/05/1916
War Diary	Stoneham Camp	02/05/1916	15/05/1916
War Diary	St. Riquier	16/05/1916	21/05/1916
War Diary	Hesmond	22/05/1916	24/06/1916
War Diary	On The March	25/06/1916	26/06/1916
War Diary	Bonnay	27/06/1916	04/07/1916
War Diary	Allery	05/07/1916	08/07/1916
War Diary	Corbie	09/07/1916	09/07/1916
War Diary	Vaux Sur Somme	10/07/1916	19/07/1916
War Diary	La-Neuville	20/07/1916	01/08/1916
War Diary	Soues	02/08/1916	02/08/1916
War Diary	Neuf Moulin	03/08/1916	04/08/1916
War Diary	Maintenay	05/08/1916	05/08/1916
War Diary	Hesmond	06/08/1916	10/08/1916
War Diary	Royon	11/08/1916	31/08/1916
Heading	War Diary. North Somerset Yeomanry 1st to 30th September 1916 Vol 17		
War Diary	Royon	01/09/1916	10/09/1916
War Diary	Saulchoy	11/09/1916	11/09/1916
War Diary	Neuilly L'Hopital	12/09/1916	12/09/1916
War Diary	La Chaussee	13/09/1916	14/09/1916
War Diary	Bussy-les-Daours	15/09/1916	15/09/1916

War Diary	Bonnay	16/09/1916	18/09/1916
War Diary	Pont Noyelles	19/09/1916	22/09/1916
War Diary	Soues	23/09/1916	23/09/1916
War Diary	Bealcourt	24/09/1916	24/09/1916
War Diary	Saulchoy	25/09/1916	29/09/1916
War Diary	Merlimont Plage	30/09/1916	30/09/1916
Heading	War Diary. North Somerset Yeomanry 1st to 31st October 1916 Vol.18		
War Diary	Merlimont Plage	01/10/1916	31/10/1916
Heading	War Diary North Somerset Yeomanry 1st to 30th November 1916 Vol.19		
War Diary	Merlimont Plage	01/11/1916	30/11/1916
Heading	War Diary North Somerset Yeomanry 1st-31st December 1916 Vol 20		
War Diary	Merlimont Plage (in billets)	01/12/1916	20/12/1916
War Diary	Offin (in billets)	22/12/1916	25/12/1916
War Diary	Offin (Pas de Calais)	01/01/1917	30/01/1917
Heading	War Diary North Somerset Yeomanry 1st to 28th February 1917 Vol No 28		
War Diary	Offin	01/02/1917	28/02/1917
Heading	War Diary North Somerset Yeomanry 1st to 31st March, 1917 Volume No. 29		
War Diary	Offin	01/03/1917	27/03/1917
Heading	War Diary. North Somerset Yeomanry 1st to 30th April 1917 Vol No 30		
War Diary	Offin	01/04/1917	05/04/1917
War Diary	Nubin St Vaast	07/04/1917	07/04/1917
War Diary	Fortel	08/04/1917	08/04/1917
War Diary	Fosseux	09/04/1917	16/04/1917
War Diary	La Broye	17/04/1917	19/04/1917
War Diary	Nampont St Martin	22/04/1917	12/05/1917
War Diary	Douriez	13/05/1917	13/05/1917
War Diary	Villers L'Hopital	14/05/1917	14/05/1917
War Diary	Halloy-Les-Pernois	15/05/1917	15/05/1917
War Diary	La Neuville	16/05/1917	17/05/1917
War Diary	Bayonvillers	18/05/1917	19/05/1917
War Diary	Buire	20/05/1917	24/05/1917
War Diary	Epehy	25/05/1917	30/05/1917
Heading	War Diary North Somerset Yeomanry 1st to 30th June 1917 Vol No 32		
War Diary	Buire	01/06/1917	30/06/1917
War Diary	Reference Map 570 S.E. 1/20,000	01/06/1917	02/06/1917
War Diary	Reference Map Sheet 57c. S.E.	11/06/1917	20/06/1917
War Diary	Lieut-Colonel	21/06/1917	28/06/1917
Heading	War Diary. North Somerset Yeomanry 1st to 31st July 1917 Vol No 33		
War Diary	Buire	01/07/1917	03/07/1917
War Diary	Suzanne	04/07/1917	04/07/1917
War Diary	Heilly	05/07/1917	05/07/1917
War Diary	Authieule	06/07/1917	06/07/1917
War Diary	Etree-Wamin	07/07/1917	07/07/1917
War Diary	La Pugnoy	08/07/1917	16/07/1917
War Diary	Haverskerque	17/07/1917	31/07/1917
Heading	War Diary North Somerset Yeomanry 1st to 31st August 1917 Vol No 34		
War Diary	Haverskerque	01/08/1917	31/08/1917

Heading	War Diary North Somerset Yeomanry 1st to 30th September 1917 Vol No 35		
War Diary	Haverskerque	01/09/1917	30/09/1917
Heading	War Diary North Somerset Yeomanry 1st to 31st October 1917 Vol No 36		
War Diary	Haverskerque	01/10/1917	19/10/1917
War Diary	Valhuon	20/10/1917	22/10/1917
War Diary	Sericourt	23/10/1917	23/10/1917
War Diary	Bonneville	24/10/1917	24/10/1917
War Diary	Limeux	25/10/1917	28/10/1917
War Diary	Eaucourt	29/10/1917	31/10/1917
Heading	War Diary. North Somerset Yeomanry 1st to 30th November 1917 Vol No. 37		
War Diary	Eaucourt	01/11/1917	17/11/1917
War Diary	Behencourt	18/11/1917	18/11/1917
War Diary	Cappy	19/11/1917	23/11/1917
War Diary	Contay	24/11/1917	30/11/1917
Heading	War Diary. North Somerset Yeomanry 1st. to 31st December 1917 Vol No 38		
War Diary	Contay	01/12/1917	21/12/1917
War Diary	Long	22/12/1917	28/01/1918
War Diary	Picquigny	29/01/1918	29/01/1918
War Diary	Bayonvillers	30/01/1918	30/01/1918
War Diary	Tertry	31/01/1918	31/01/1918
Heading	War Diary North Somerset Yeomanry 1st to 28th February 1918 Vol No 40		
War Diary	Tertry	01/02/1918	28/02/1918
Heading	War Diary North Somerset Yeomanry 1st to 31st March 1918 Vol No 41 6 Bde 3 Cav Div		
War Diary	Tertry	01/03/1918	13/03/1918
War Diary	Brie	14/03/1918	14/03/1918
War Diary	Airhines	15/03/1918	26/03/1918
War Diary	L'Etoile	27/03/1918	31/03/1918

(4)

WO 95/1153

3 Cavalry Division

6 Cavalry Brigade

1/1 North Somerset Yeomanry

Nov 1914 - Mar. 1918

1914-1918
3RD CAVALRY DIVISION
6TH CAVALRY BRIGADE.

NORTH SOMERSET YEOMANRY
NOV 1914 - MAR 1918

NORTH

SOMERSET

YEOMANRY

November to December 1914

Vol 1.

Mar 1918

WAR DIARY
INTELLIGENCE SUMMARY.
(Erase heading not required.)

Army Form C. 2118.

Instructions regarding War Diaries and Intelligence Summaries are contained in F.S. Regs., Part II. and the Staff Manual respectively. Title pages will be prepared in manuscript.

Hour, Date, Place	Summary of Events and Information	Remarks and references to Appendices
2-xi-14 FOREST ROW	The regiment strength 26 officers 1 warrant officer and 474 other ranks with 500 horses under the command of Lt Col G.C. GLYN D.S.O. left FOREST ROW in 4 special trains for SOUTHAMPTON where it embarked during the evening on S.S. ROSETTI.	5.5 am ?
3-xi-14 AT SEA	The ROSETTI reached HAVRE at 3 pm and the regiment disembarked, moved off at 6 pm to a rest camp at LA HÈVE 2½ miles N.W. of HAVRE. The transport wagons did not leave the dock till 8 am.	Transport App. I
4-xi-14 LA HÈVE	In the morning the regt was inspected by the base commandant and Col H.B. WILLIAMS D.S.O. The rest consisted its equipment from Ordnance. 5 wagons received from DEPOT FORD on 1-xi-14 having become unserviceable were changed.	Equipment. App II
5-xi-14 LA HÈVE	The regt received orders to entrain for ST OMER and left in 3 special trains between 3.45pm & 6.45pm	
6-xi-14 ON RAIL	The regt arrived at ST OMER & spent the night in FRENCH ARTILLERY BARRACKS there	Billets. App. III
7-xi-14 ST OMER	The regt paraded at 10.30 AM and were led to its billeting area in and around ESQUERDES. The men in sheds	Billets. App III
8-xi-14 ESQUERDES	In the afternoon the regt was practised in digging trenches	

WAR DIARY
INTELLIGENCE SUMMARY.
(Erase heading not required.)

Army Form C. 2118.

Instructions regarding War Diaries and Intelligence Summaries are contained in F. S. Regs., Part II. and the Staff Manual respectively. Title pages will be prepared in manuscript.

Hour, Date, Place	Summary of Events and Information	Remarks and references to Appendices
9-xi-14 ESQUERDES	The regt paraded at 11.30 am for drill. 1 Officer & 2 N.C.O.s per Sqdn under Maj. A.M. Gibbs went to BLENDECQUES to see the entrenchments being made there	2 Sqdn, Yeo
10-xi-14 ESQUERDES	The regt paraded at 8.15 am & went to BLENDECQUES & took part in the entrenching scheme. It returned at 2.30 pm	
11-xi-14 ESQUERDES	The regt paraded for drill at 8.15 am. At 10.10 am while the regt was still at the field orders were received to march at once to billets around ST SYLVESTRE. An officer (Capt. J.H.S. Tyssen) was sent on a motor bicycle to report to G.O.C. 1st Army Corps at CHATEAU DETROUTAURS VLAMERTINGHE for orders. The regt marched at 1 pm & billeted that night in 3 farms close to ST SYLVESTRE arriving about 8.45 pm. The night was wet & stormy. The horses were in the open. Capt Tyssen brought orders to proceed to MOOSE without his reaching the regt.	Billets app III
12-xi-14 ST SYLVESTRE	The regt marched to DRANOUTRE at 10 am via BAILLEUL arriving there at 2.30 pm and billeting in 4 farms, the horses were in the open. The water for horses was not good. The regt's arrival was reported to G.O.C. 1st A. Corps.	
13-xi-14 DRANOUTRE	Acting on orders from G.O.C. 1st A. Corps the regt marched at 10.30 am to YPRES via LOCRE and DICKEBUSCH to YPRES Railway Stn & thence along the railway to HALTE on the MENIN ROAD. The regt's arrival was reported to G.O.C. 3rd Cavalry Division. The regt was posted to the 6th Cavalry Bde. The regt went into billets in a chateau next to L'ECOLE DE BIENFAISANCE	

Army Form C. 2118.

WAR DIARY
or
INTELLIGENCE SUMMARY.
(Erase heading not required.)

Instructions regarding War Diaries and Intelligence Summaries are contained in F.S. Regs., Part II. and the Staff Manual respectively. Title pages will be prepared in manuscript.

Hour, Date, Place	Summary of Events and Information	Remarks and references to Appendices
13-xi-14 DRANOOTRE (continued)	on the MENIN ROAD ½ mile E. of HALTE. While the reg.t was coming along the railway it was shelled. In there billets the horses were tied up round the side of the field. The reg.t was ordered to proceed to the trenches near ZILLEBEKE and the support and marched at 4 p.m. the men carried 200 rounds per man. On arrival the reg.t halted for an hour and just being received for duty returned to billets. The billets were shelled during the day and night several shells falling amongst the horses which however escaped without injury.	A. Som. Yeo
14-xi-14 YPRES	During the night the billets were shelled so the reg.t saddled up at 3.30 a.m. & marched at day light to the railway just N. of HALTE on the MENIN R.d. The horses were tied along the W. side of the cutting & the men made small dugouts on the E side. Like on the 13th remained in billets At 1 p.m. the Bde. received orders to march to a billeting area near VLAMERTINGHE. The reg.t was billeted in 2 farms. The billets were very cramped & the water supply bad. The weather was cold & the horses not being under shelter felt it. The reg.t was warned to find 300 rifles for the trenches on 15-xi-14 to 48 hours	
15-xi-14 VLAMERTINGHE	Orders were received at 2.45 a.m. The reg.t paraded dismounted at 3.30 a.m. & marched 200 round An the reg.t Bde. under Col (C) near YPRES railway station at war. The B. Squadron under Maj. H.G. Spencer, was ordered to join the 10th Hussars. A. Sqdn under Maj. Loubouck Bordn under Capt. F.A.C. Lisbert and B Sqdn under Maj. H.G. Mathews were placed under the orders of Col. a. The Maxims under Maj. Bingham D.S.O. 3rd D.G.s & told to occupy the trenches S.E. of ZILLEBEKE On arrival at ZILLEBEKE C sqdn under Maj. Loubrock Borden under Capt. F.A.C. Lisbert and

SMITH, BINGHAM D.S.O.

WAR DIARY
INTELLIGENCE SUMMARY.
(Erase heading not required.)

Army Form C. 2118.

Hour, Date, Place	Summary of Events and Information	Remarks and references to Appendices
15-xi-14 VLAMERTINGHE (continued)	The relief of the 1st LIFE G'ds was effected at 7.30 p.m. A SQDN occupied the centre trench in the firing line with the maxims between 2 SQDNS & 3rd D.G. B SQDN was in the reserve trenches. The night 15/16 – was fairly quiet but there was a certain amount of intermittent shelling & sniping & a small attack which was easily repulsed.	2. Somr Jam.
16-xi-14 ZILLEBEKE	During the day there was continuous shelling and sniping and a few casualties from shrapnel. At 6.30 p.m. B SQDN and one troop of A SQDN under 2/Lt N. BARNARD relieved A SQDN which went into the reserve trenches. The maxim guns stayed in the firing line. There was a small attack about 9 p.m. which was easily repulsed.	
17-xi-14 ZILLEBEKE	9 a.m. Heavy shelling started & the trenches were searched by shrapnel & H.E. shell, which gave off repulsive fumes. 2 GERMAN aeroplanes passed up the lines followed by a 3rd. The trenches had already been damaged by shell fire & no R.E. were available. They were repaired by the men as best they could but owing to the softness of the soil & no materials for revetting being available the trenches were soon rendered valueless again. A determined attack was made at noon which was repulsed with heavy loss causing the ag. many casualties including Capt LIEBERT who was killed. The attack was renewed and BRIG GEN. LORD CAVAN was now informed and asked for reinforcements. He sent up 2 Coys COLDSTREAM G'ds who occupied the reserve trenches at 3.30 p.m. Meanwhile the attack had been continued and LT J.S. DAVEY killed. 30 men of A SQDN were sent up under CAPT R.E. ENGLISH to take place casualties	

WAR DIARY / INTELLIGENCE SUMMARY

Army Form C. 2118.

Hour, Date, Place	Summary of Events and Information	Remarks and references to Appendices
17-xi-14 ZILLEBEKE	Late in the remainder of A Sqdn under Major GLUBBOCK was sent up. The enemy made another determined attack at dusk but were repulsed with heavy loss mainly it is unnecessary to call up the COLDSTREAM GDS. The enemy sent up a balloon at midday with flares attached & in the evening used magnesium light to blind the attack. The relief of the trenches was carried out at 6.30 pm by the 2nd LIFE GDS in the firing line and R.HORSE GDS in reserve. C Sqdn came under heavy shell fire in the reserve trenches but did not occupy the front trenches. The rest were dismounted to YPRES where it picked up its horses & returned to billets near VLAMERTINGHE. CASUALTIES — CAPT. F.G.C. LIEBERT and Lt. J.S. DAVEY Killed CAPT. S.G. BATES 7th HUSSARS (ADJT) and 2Lt AM BAILWARD Wounded 3 N.C.O.S. and men Killed 22 Wounded 39 missing 3. Total casualties 64. Out of these 59 were sustained to by the 200 officers in trenches at ZILLEBEKE. The weather had been bitterly cold the last few days & the horses suffered from exposure	J. Som. Yeo Points VII
18-19-xi-14 VLAMERTINGHE	The rest remained in billets	

Army Form C. 2118.

(6)

WAR DIARY
or
INTELLIGENCE SUMMARY.
(Erase heading not required.)

Instructions regarding War Diaries and Intelligence Summaries are contained in F.S. Regs., Part II. and the Staff Manual respectively. Title pages will be prepared in manuscript.

Hour, Date, Place	Summary of Events and Information	Remarks and references to Appendices
20-xi-14 VLAMERTINGHE	The transport moved off at 7.30 am and the Brigade at 3 pm to a billeting area to just NE MERVILLE. The roads were very slippery owing to frost and the regt did not reach its billets till between 12 & 2 am. Each sqdn and the Maximum gun occupied group of farms & well Hd Quarters were established at the CHATEAU BUTOT ¾ mile NE MERVILLE on the HAZEBROUCK Rd. All the limbers were placed under cover.	2.5 am Frost
21-xii-14 MERVILLE	The regt remained in billets & continued training. In the regt was set in horseman-ship training. S.A.A. Echelon "A" was reorganised into 2/portions of 2 limbered wagons for Cols & S.A.A. Echelon "A" was reorganised into 2/portions of "MOBILE" consisting of 2 limbered wagons (drawn from M. Gun section) replaced by local horses "IMMOBILE" 2 G.S. WAGONS Med Cart Water Cart & 1 pair Horse draught Limber	Billets
13-xii-14 6.	The colonial pattern saddle with which the regt was equipped was found to be too narrow in the front arch to allow of a blanket being carried under the saddle & authority was obtained to assume issue U.P. saddles in exchange.	
14 xii-14 MERVILLE	The regt paraded with the Brigade at 7.15 am and marched to a position NE BAILLEUL. The whole of the 6th & 7th Brigades were concentrated there. At 2 pm the regt returned to billets in BAILLEUL. The horses were tied up in the open & the men were put in flour-stores ¼ mile away.	
15-xii-14 BAILLEUL	The regt did not leave billets	

Army Form C. 2118.
(7)

WAR DIARY
INTELLIGENCE SUMMARY.
(Erase heading not required.)

Instructions regarding War Diaries and Intelligence Summaries are contained in F.S. Regs., Part II. and the Staff Manual respectively. Title pages will be prepared in manuscript.

Hour, Date, Place	Summary of Events and Information	Remarks and references to Appendices
16-xii-14 BAILLEUL	The regt marched at 8.30am & returned with the Brigade to its original billets near MERVILLE	2 Scan/Foo
17-xii – 19-xii-14 MERVILLE	The regt remained in billets & continued training	
20-xii-14	The regt received orders at 4 pm to be ready to move at any & hot notice. This order was cancelled at 7.30 pm.	
21-22-xii-14 MERVILLE	The regt remained in billets and continued training	
23-xii-14 MERVILLE	A draft of 2 officers (Capt W.S. BATTEN-POOLL & Lt W.D. WILLS) and 25 N.C.Os and men arrived. The war office issued authority for the Regt. to be made up to Establishment Gtr	Strength APP IV
24-27-xii-14 MERVILLE	The regt remained in billets and continued training.	S
28-xii-14 MERVILLE	Information was received that the regt was to be raised from Yeomanry to CAVALRY establishment to ensure an increase of 73 horses and 172 horses	
29-31-xii-14 MERVILLE	The regt remained in billets and continued training	

121/4559

6th Cavalry Brigade
S/17

Intelligence Germany

Vol II 1st Jan.
28.2.15

Appendix I — Unsuitable water supplied to horses —

Army Form C. 2118.

WAR DIARY
or
INTELLIGENCE SUMMARY.
(Erase heading not required.)

Instructions regarding War Diaries and Intelligence Summaries are contained in F.S. Regs., Part II. and the Staff Manual respectively. Title pages will be prepared in manuscript.

Hour, Date, Place	Summary of Events and Information	Remarks and references to Appendices
1.1.15 to 9.1.15. MERVILLE	The Regiment remain in billets and continue training. The weather was wet. Lt R. Chiodi took over control of the Brigade M.G. course.	
10.1.15 to 12.1.15. MERVILLE	The Regiment remain in billets. A machine gun course under Lt Holt & Lt Lee took no survivors. 9 men detailed.	2nd Scots Guards
13.1.15.	Major Leonard J. Payne on inspected the supplies of the regiment.	
14.1.15 to 16.1.15. MERVILLE	Regiment engaged in fatigues, training etc. Major General J. Byng inspected the Machine Gun detachment at 2nd Division headquarters at Hazebrouck. 16.1.15	
17.1.15 to 19.1.15. MERVILLE	Regiment remain in billets and continue training. 9 N.C.O.s & 15 reported to their division possible 3 corporals made up to Lance Corporal. Brigade route march by "B" Echelon.	
20.1.15 to 24.1.15. MERVILLE	Regimental Route march. Trench digging by night party to man waggon passed the O.C. 9th Bn in John Ford inspected and addressed the regiment.	
25.1.15.	The Brigade moves billets to STEENBECQUE Division pontoon reserve to Brigade	

WAR DIARY
or
INTELLIGENCE SUMMARY.
(Erase heading not required.)

Army Form C. 2118.

9.

Instructions regarding War Diaries and Intelligence Summaries are contained in F.S. Regs., Part II. and the Staff Manual respectively. Title pages will be prepared in manuscript.

Hour, Date, Place	Summary of Events and Information	Remarks and references to Appendices
29.1.15 to 31.1.15 STEENBECQUE	Staff of 10 Officers and 7 S.S. other ranks arrived from Rouen + one Coy Regiment settling into new billets	App III Billets. App IV Strength
1.2.15 STEENBECQUE	Regiment resting in billets.	
2.2.15 STEENBECQUE	Schloss H. and H.gun of 4th Brigade marched to Pouperinghe and Ypres. Billeting party under Captain G.L. Gibbs joined Headquarters and Preceded by Motor bus into reminder of Brigade billeting party to YPRES.	
3.2.15 STEENBECQUE	Brigade paraded at 2 p.m. and Embussed for YPRES when the Regiment went into billets. Strength 30 Officers 226 O.R. + 2 machine guns.	App. III Billets
4.2.15 YPRES	Regiment in billets. Shells fell during night and aeroplane dropped two bombs on the short list did no damage. One officer and 25 men went to trenches for 24 hours.	
5.2.15 YPRES	Regiment in billets. Supplies brought up daily from Poperinghe where Schloss H. was billeted. Shells fell on town. Other Squadron leader and one officer for situation went to trenches for 24 hours.	

Signed [illegible signature] Lt Col
2 Coy 4/Dr

Army Form C. 2118.

10

WAR DIARY
or
INTELLIGENCE SUMMARY.
(Erase heading not required.)

Instructions regarding War Diaries and Intelligence Summaries are contained in F. S. Regs., Part II. and the Staff Manual respectively. Title pages will be prepared in manuscript.

Hour, Date, Place	Summary of Events and Information	Remarks and references to Appendices
6.2.15 YPRES.	C.O's and N.A. Officers went to trenches for 24 hours. Regiment in billets. Weather wet.	
7.2.15. N pm	Regiment in billets. Coy and one Officer per squadron went to trenches for 24 hours and reported weather wet.	
8.2.15. YPRES.	Regiment marched at 8.30 pm to trenches and took them over. 3rd D. in reserve 2nd left Greaves. N. Somerset Yeomanry the Leicestershire Yeomanry. 3rd Royal Dragoons in 1st Line Greaves. The relief effected satisfactorily by 10 pm and without casualty. The trenches fairly dry but in places very wet. Dugouts not sufficient for the number of officers.	9.30 pm Guy Hutton Lt Col

Forms/C. 2118/10

Army Form C. 2118.

WAR DIARY
or
INTELLIGENCE SUMMARY.
(Erase heading not required.)

Hour, Date, Place	Summary of Events and Information	Remarks and references to Appendices
9.2.15. TRENCHES.	The Regiment in trenches. Considerable sniping - Some men employed in strengthening trenches. Sandbags filled - Wire drawn up in front [ ] German shells are in rear of C Oi dug out station wires. S.Q.M.S. D Miller wounded at JILLEBEKE while obtaining rations. [Weather wet]	
10.2.15 TRENCHES.	Continued sniping and shelling of same area for 1½ hours. Weather wet. No casualties. Both continue improving themselves. French guns 75 mm. shelters enemy trenches for us - shooting very accurate. New gun emplaced.	
11.2.15 TRENCHES.	A bad night - Dead manual sniping and firing. In early morning - Continued sniping and shelling of same area. Casualties. Captain Euston L Gibbs killed. Pte. S.C. Stone killed. One O.R. wounded.	

WAR DIARY
or
INTELLIGENCE SUMMARY.
(Erase heading not required.)

Army Form C. 2118.

12

Hour, Date, Place	Summary of Events and Information	Remarks and references to Appendices
12.2.15 TRENCHES	Cold night. Some snow. Trench bombs thrown but did not turn any on - but destroyed parapets which were repaired. Hand grenade thrown and S.S.M. W. REEVES picked up our unbroken fuse thrown boomerang. Strong & taking area. Shepherd wounded some men. 3 O.R wounded by Shrapnel 1. O.R. " " bullet. Officers from Relief brigade came up & knew trenches.	N Somme yer [signature] Lutty Jug Col
13.2.15	Wet morning. Continuous sniping and shelling. Relief took place at 4 p.m. And something tended our satisfactory. Regiment marched back under squadron leaders to YPRES where was inside by 3.30. a.m. of 14th.	

Army Form C. 2118.

13.

WAR DIARY
or
INTELLIGENCE SUMMARY.
(Erase heading not required.)

Instructions regarding War Diaries and Intelligence Summaries are contained in F.S. Regs., Part II. and the Staff Manual respectively. Title pages will be prepared in manuscript.

Hour, Date, Place	Summary of Events and Information	Remarks and references to Appendices
14.2.15. Ypres → STEEN BECQUE	Regiment embussed at 3.30 am and reached Ebleute at 7 am	
15.2.15. STEEN BECQUE	Regiment in billets - Cavalry work recommenced. Buses again offered. Heavy repairs - Walsh honourably invalided	
16.2.15. STEEN BECQUE	Regiment in billets. Visit by General Allenby and staff.	
18.2.15. STEEN BECQUE 19.2.15.	Regiment in billets. A batch of 75 remounts arrive from Rouen. Inspection by Lt Gen Allenby (GOC 3rd Cav. Division) and Commdg. Brig. Swell - by General Allenby who inspected then and Brig. Genl. D Campbell.	

Forms/C. 2118/10

Army Form C. 2118.

WAR DIARY
or
INTELLIGENCE SUMMARY.
(Erase heading not required.)

Instructions regarding War Diaries and Intelligence Summaries are contained in F. S. Regs., Part II. and the Staff Manual respectively. Title pages will be prepared in manuscript.

Hour, Date, Place	Summary of Events and Information	Remarks and references to Appendices
20.2.15. STEENBECQUE	Regiment in billets. Remounts again inspected by Brig Genl Campbell and one youth and horse to inspection of 9 R Lrs.	
21.2.15. STEENBECQUE	General Parade. Capt Paul for Indian Army Corps selected Six remounts as suitable for pack forms. Strength 4 sqns 5 R's and armoured fully equipped and mounted	Aph. IV Strength.
22.2.15. STEENBECQUE	Regiment in billets. Cavalry training continued including Squadron exercises under the new pattern sword. breathing starting - but acre some corners.	N. Somme
26.2.15.	Route marches and tactical schemes - troops approach Steenpis out.	

Hubert Gough per
N.H.Tomaine Young

APPEN.DIX   Transport
I

The S.S. Rosetti on which the Regiment was conveyed to Havre was a well found boat and the accommodation for the horses good. The gangways were of well provided.

The means of disembarkation at Havre was not of such a nature as to make for quick disembarkation. The gang work the Engineers for unloading the waggons was hardly sufficient.

The water for the horses on board was not satisfactory because it had been standing in tubs for some time and I attribute to it a certain amount of sickness a short time after the landing.

                                             Geoffrey Glyn.
                                                   Lt.Col.

Appendix   Equipment
   II

Just prior to the departure of the Regiment from Forest Row, the transport establishment was increased and waggons issued at Deptford. Two of these waggons were cast as unserviceable at Havre. The swords issued were the old pattern. But new pattern have been supplied.

Geoffrey Glyn
Lt Col

APPENDIX. III   BILLETS

S'OMER — The barracks allotted to the Regiment were the old artillery barracks and were dirty and lousy. Aufrès troops had left them uncleaned.

ESQUERDES — The regiment billeted in farms which were fairly clean but the camping ground for the horses was too low lying and unsuitable for horses just landed at that time of year — especially it would have been so had the passage been a rough one — after the bad drinking water. Straw available but hay difficult to obtain.

S. SYLVESTRE — Billets were good for the men — horses in the open. Water convenient but not very good.

VLAMERTINGHE — The billets were very confined and the men too crowded.

MERVILLE — The regiment was in billets here from 21.XI.14 to 28.1.15. The squadrons were in various farms and the men housed comfortably in farms. The horses were all under cover, but the numerous chickens about produced a certain amount of lice. The horses of the farmers were not all healthy. Sanitation is very primitive, but the health of the men kept good. The horses were good. Straw and fresh vegetables in good quantities. Hay could only be obtained with difficulty.

Appendix III   Billets

STEENBEECQ   The billets satisfactory – inhabitants on the whole agreeable. The situation higher and more healthy.
Farms a little scattered.

YPRES.   The regiment was billeted in empty houses or partly inhabited – but many partially destroyed – and in empty half destroyed schools. The water supply was insanitary and all water was drawn in the water cart from the batteries where proper supervision was maintained by the R.A.M.C.

Geoffrey Glyn
Lt Col
N.S.W.

Appendix. IV   Strength.

1st Draft — 2 officers and 25 men. This was not satisfactory. the men were not well trained and not good physique. few went sick in a week after arrival. The horses were a good stamp.

2nd Draft — One Officer: 75 men. This draft arrived in January. The men were a good lot and smart but not trained in riding. Their private vocations various: but all keen and intelligent. This draft came fully equipped but dismounted.

Remounts. Seventy five remounts were sent up on Feb. 17. but of a very small size. R.D.2. They were none of them really suited to cavalry work — though of their stamp good. but more suited to pack pony work. Some very weak — and many lousy.

3rd Draft — This draft of 52 men arrived on Feb. 21. Mounted and fully equipped. a keen intelligent lot of men but not much trained in riding. The horses were more of the cavalry type than the last draft. Many were unseens and some very weak. Some were unfit for work from inefficient causes.

The question of drafts is a difficult one for Yeomanry: many men are taken on the strength whose constitutions will not stand a hard campaign. and thus become a burden on the State.

Appendix IV Cont'd

Remounts
Draft of 59 Remounts arrived on April 13th. A useful lot of horses.

Strength
Major Bramwell left regiment to take command of XV. Hussars brigaded in 9th Brig with 19th Hussars and subsequently Bedford Yeomanry.

Strength
Major H. Gibbs left to command 3rd Regiment April 21st

Strength
Major R. Campbell 14th Hussars joined as 2nd in Command

Strength
Draft of 73 O.R. arrived from England. These men were in many cases quite untrained in riding & it was with great advantage N.C.O's often 3rd D.G. & "Royals" were lent to train the men, who quickly learnt as they have been.

June 1915

Strength
Capt. W. L. Kirby of the 12th Lancers, & from the Shropshire Yeomanry joined as adjutant July 1915

Major F. B. N. Dunn West. Cant'd Yeo'y
— C. Dewhurst Lanc. Hussars.
Capt. R. A. West. N. Irish Horse.
Lieut. G. Babington. Left Forfar Yeo'y
2/Lt. R. B. Green 7/ N.S.Y
— L. Fry 7/ N.S.Y
— Tisdale 7/ N.S.Y
— Corrie " "
Lt. Col. M. R. Backhouse North'd Hussars.
Do.

} These officers joined in turn to replace casualties.

6th Cavalry Brigade

Centre Frances Germany
Vol II 1 — 31.3.15.

Army Form C. 2118.

WAR DIARY
or
INTELLIGENCE SUMMARY.
(Erase heading not required.)

Instructions regarding War Diaries and Intelligence Summaries are contained in F.S. Regs., Part II. and the Staff Manual respectively. Title pages will be prepared in manuscript.

Hour, Date, Place	Summary of Events and Information	Remarks and references to Appendices
1.3.15 STEENBECQUE	Intelled	
2.3.15 - 6. 4.3.15 STEENBECQUE	Intelled. Preparing Transport. Trn Case of Meningitis sent to hospital. C.S.M Grand's S.S.M. Reserve Wagon 3ʳᵈ Grenat S.S.M. Reserve Cann to congratulate R.S.M. Strahope in turn. D.C. to examine.	
5.3.15 6. 9.3.15 STEENBECQUE	Intelled. Regiment cold turn of duty digging trenches. Took one case.	
9.3.15 and 10.3.15 STEENBECQUE	Fine but cold. Brigade Route March. Private ordered release to bury 4 horn. C.O's conference with Brigadier.	
11.3.15 - 12	Reveille 6.20 a.m. 15 camel bridge on MERVIH-17- LA MOTTE road - Killer at day. Heavy firing to our front. NEUVE-ETAPARPRE. Melville in ose ams near MERVILLE as ambulance cases to 1ˢᵗ Army who we engage	
13.3.15 MERVILLE	Relieved remains at Steenbecque - The Cavalry Corps are also moved to men the Arr. arsent. Store to all day mist rain shown at one hour interval. Ring firing	
14.3.15 - 6	Sin on. The Aunnibis had officers laut to the Kitap Killer - Many gunner Ammunn taken 13ᵗʰ 11ᵗʰ Jayes Regt. Principal return to Ireland. Brittle fins had front dead Advance been on right of 13ᵗʰ as STEENBECQUE. of unit.	

Muffry Flyn
Lt Col N Somerset

Army Form C. 2118
2

WAR DIARY
or
INTELLIGENCE SUMMARY.
(Erase heading not required.)

Instructions regarding War Diaries and Intelligence Summaries are contained in F. S. Regs., Part II. and the Staff Manual respectively. Title pages will be prepared in manuscript.

Hour, Date, Place	Summary of Events and Information	Remarks and references to Appendices
14.3.15 - 16.3.15 STEENBECQUE	Fine but duller and rather cold. Very heavy gun fire audible. Saddlers ordered to trim & turn in at times ranges from 10 am to mid to noon. Major Cooper rejoined. 2 Dr in Lee & Byza inspected and authorised to leave.	
17.3.15 - 31.3.15	Dr Mellis. Weather very variable. Some Snow. Training of Regiment Continue - Tactical Scheme under G.O.C. Brigade. Map Sketch exercises. Cadres of horses to 2ⁿᵈ Army and Remounts arrive from Rouen. The Remounts are a fine Class of Cavalry horse. One officer and six O.R. parties from Base with horses and equipment Issue orders issue of payment for billets -	[signature] Guthrey Feege Lt Col N. Som Yeomanry

3rd Cavalry Division

121/6356

North Irish Horse.

Vol III

Army Form C. 2118.

WAR DIARY
or
INTELLIGENCE SUMMARY.
(Erase heading not required.)

Instructions regarding War Diaries and Intelligence Summaries are contained in F. S. Regs., Part II. and the Staff Manual respectively. Title pages will be prepared in manuscript.

Hour, Date, Place	Summary of Events and Information	Remarks and references to Appendices
1.4.15 — STEENBECQUE	In billets. A course of instruction in trench carrier on at Hazebrouck. Also a course on trench mortar firing.	
2.4.15. STEENBECQUE	In billets. A draft of 50 men and horses arrived from 2/1 W. Somt. Regt. This brought the Regiment up to Cavalry strength for the first time in its history.	
3.4.15 - 6.4.15 STEENBECQUE	In billets. Troop leaders scheme under C.O. & Imberget — At RE Colonel Bates selected 12 horses for 2nd Army horses wd.—	
7.4.15 to STEENBECQUE 12.4.15	Inspection by G.O.C.A., General D. Campbell and 2/Lieut. Sir S. Bryce, West. Some snow. The Win on complimentary. Divisional order issued at WALLON CAPPEL changing billets in order to make room for Royal Horse Artillery.	App IV
13.4.15 to STEENBECQUE 17.4.15	54 Remounts arrived to R.B. Price M.O. Oyr. Regt. and to R.O'Kelly joined. 2/Lt. R Withers on B.F. 1000 joined for Rouen. 1 Om. D.R., Q.S.C. Brig. Gen. D. Campbell, promoted D.C.M. & S.S.M. to Reserve. Field day with Regt. on 14. with 3td Bryp. on 16th	App IV
	Lt Gaston Warrender with Bomb.	
	Weather changeable	[signature] Lt. Col.

(9 29 6) W 4141—463 100,000 9/14 H W V Forms/C. 2118/10

Army Form C. 2118.

WAR DIARY
or
INTELLIGENCE SUMMARY.
(Erase heading not required.)

Instructions regarding War Diaries and Intelligence Summaries are contained in F.S. Regs., Part II. and the Staff Manual respectively. Title pages will be prepared in manuscript.

Hour, Date, Place	Summary of Events and Information	Remarks and references to Appendices
18.4.15 to 22.4.15 STEENBECQUE	In billets. Routine. Major H[?] gave home on leave & taken over command of C Squadron. Regiment. "C" Squadron isolated on account of measles. Regiment found a party to unit digging at LA BELLE HOTESSE — with Canadians.	App. IV.
23.4.15 on the march	Brigade rendezvous. 11.45 a.m. and marches to ABEELE joining the Division en mass. Heavy fighting going on — mass billets at EGERE — Eculen B. before STEENBECQUE — [struck through] Canadian Cavalry Brigade came broken [?]	
24.4.15 on the march	Marches to POPERINGHE when war was raging - to move ½ hour when orders billets in BOISCHETE. Int. Indian Brigade also in village.	
25.4.15 on the march	Marches to covert N.W. of POPERINGHE where war being raging - the front in Sire war began - inhabitants leaving town - halter and the billeted at HOUTKERQUE Fine.	
26.4.15 on the march	Marches to P.W. of POPPERINGHE till 6 p.m. to mountain park marker to VLAMERTINGHE - horse left at firm halt. Billets close near turnpike and onward march to war to take cover in cases of shelling. Fine	
27.4.15 VLAMERTINGHE and	Halted. Some heavy shelling. Many troops and lorries arriving — the new horse officer 2nd Lieut. Stampdew but Canadians lorry light prompt advice after Regent + N. Song Marchant's clearing out. Hospital when we found horse had to be evacuated. Headquarter staff of regiment left the town. The night passed quietly, but shelling began at 9 a.m. — in afternoon he reported ground to leave and billets at San Jan de BIESEN.	
28.4.15		

Forms/C. 2118/10

WAR DIARY
INTELLIGENCE SUMMARY
(Erase heading not required.)

Army Form C. 2118.

(1a)

Hour, Date, Place	Summary of Events and Information	Remarks and references to Appendices
29.4.15. On the march	Move from billets N.E. w. of POPPERINGHE - day passed quietly, heavy infantry guns away. Ann. heard fighting round YPRES. and billeted at SAN JAN de BIESEN. Lt Gaston Pluto Wormer taken ill.	
30.4.15. On the march	Move from billets to w. of POPPERINGHE. Officers ordered to go to take own trenches but order cancelled: and regiment marched to billets standing to as troops danger of reserves.	
1.5.15. On the march	Move out of billets: and after standing to was ordered night to new billets at PROVEN. Lt Ing R Gibb, N.S.Y. D'Kelly RAM Surrendered will proceed [illegible]	
2.5.15. On the march	Regiment ordered to reinforce (in afternoon) (and) went mounted to Pro. w. of POPPERINGHE - dismounted and the whole division turned was on at Proven w. of YPRES. night spent lying in plough'd field as reserve while line being straightened - (Monday) hard (a) am here of the division at (an [illegible]) horses and trans killed/at PROVEN. (Thunderstorm)	
3.5.15 PROVEN.	This Sat. May R. FISHER left to take up post on G.S.O.2 2nd Division. Capt C. Howard 1st Dragoon Grove who is wounded had marched 3.4.5.6 via POPPERINGHE and VLAMERTINGHE. The division dismounted to YPRES and dug trenches S. of YPRES under shell fire. Royals had two casualties. One Pte. COLLINS killed & Pte Smith wounded	

Army Form C. 2118.

(20)

WAR DIARY
or
INTELLIGENCE SUMMARY.

(Erase heading not required.)

Instructions regarding War Diaries and Intelligence Summaries are contained in F. S. Regs., Part II. and the Staff Manual respectively. Title pages will be prepared in manuscript.

Hour, Date, Place	Summary of Events and Information	Remarks and references to Appendices
6.5.15 PROVEN	Dismounted party-arrived home at 2 a.m. and reached billets 6 a.m. Casualties Killed. Pte COLLINS. Wounded Lt. J. A. GARTON – RSM W. SHAKESPEARE Pte BURRELL_R STREET Major R Campbell came down in better health. Blanner plan	APP IV
7.5.15 PROVEN and 8.5.15	Marched 2.30 p.m. and received STEENBECQUE 8.30 pm. – Thunder Attended Lecture I Corps. Byng Cav. Corps. Briggs. St. Omer. In cantonments – Major R Campbell returned. Back from St. Omer.	
9.5.15	Officer asked to bring troop to no billets and bus escorts. As men orders came to move at once by omnibus. Left at 10 am. to have YPRES – via ABEELE, VLAMERTINGHE. Enemy Gent, hard hitting 3rd Cavalry Div. outflank. The whole Division up. N. 34 half near BRIELEN J. – Day outside. 300 officers men – At night – hand digging. And to cover Shells and towns YPRES. Aeroplanes frequent and a couple look out posts. Prisoners at night gate. On night of 9/12 Major McAllan at garden Arrived troops, into B N C.O. now up to take over trenches – Ant	
YPRES		
10.5.15	On the night 12/13th we took over trenches at BELLEWARDE Farm road	

WAR DIARY
INTELLIGENCE SUMMARY

Army Form C. 2118.

(21)

Hour, Date, Place	Summary of Events and Information	Remarks and references to Appendices
13.5.15 YPRES	Took over trenches at 11 p.m. under heavy shrapnel fire. Casualties on the move up. The whole area subjected to very heavy shell fire. The right of the line was occupied by the N.S.Y. on their right in the same of the road were the 8th Royal Irish Cav. & Roulers; on the left of the N.S.Y. the 3rd D. Gds. - the Burgade in reserve 700 yards in rear. Seven positions reached 1.15 a.m. in front. Attle left of the 3rd D. Gds. was 7th Brigade and at POTIJZE in support the 8th. Position heavy bombardment commenced at 3.45 a.m. and continued throughout the day. German attacks as yet, but were repulsed with heavy loss. Continuous violent bombardment, at intervals severe attacks. 7th Brigade lost their trenches and a counter attack by 8th Brigade regained the position. Violent bombardment till night when reports reliefs came up. The guns on our side made no effective reply as the brigade of his action. Heavy casualties in the whole	

WAR DIARY
or
INTELLIGENCE SUMMARY.
(Erase heading not required.)

Army Form C. 2118.

(22)

Hour, Date, Place	Summary of Events and Information	Remarks and references to Appendices

13.5.15. (continue) YPRES.	Brigade. killed. wounded. Total.
	N.S.Y. 3 + 25 8 + 100. 125 –
	3rd D.G.
	1st Royals
	Brig. Hqrs.
	
	Officers of N.S.Y. killed. Major R. Crawford
	                                          Capt. E. Inglis.
	                                          Capt. S.G. Bath –
	                         wounded. Lt.Col. G.C. Glyn DSO.
	                                          Major St. Spencer
	                                          Major G. Littock.
	                                          Major W.O. Matthews
	                                          Lt. G.G. Longruss
	                                          Lt. L.C. Gibbs
	                                          Lt. B.2. Hogg
	                                          Lt. R. Wilson	

Army Form C. 2118.

23

WAR DIARY
or
INTELLIGENCE SUMMARY.
(Erase heading not required.)

Instructions regarding War Diaries and Intelligence Summaries are contained in F.S. Regs., Part II. and the Staff Manual respectively. Title pages will be prepared in manuscript.

Hour, Date, Place	Summary of Events and Information	Remarks and references to Appendices
13.5.15 Cont'd. YPRES	At night the regiment was relieved. Lt. J.G. Paxton awarded the Militia Cross. Sergt. Cham hit Gun —	
14.5.15. YPRES	The Regiment took over the reserve trenches at POTIZE and returned to VLAMERTINGHE on h—	
15.5.15 to 22.5.15 VLAMERTINGHE	15th remains there to move up as short notice Capt. R. Homoth 1st Royals late Lieutenant command The Regiment remained as No.1 Mobile Reserve at VLAMERTINGHE	
23.5.15 to 28.5.15 Lt.Col 7?.7? STEENBECQUE	In our billets. Machine gun course. Lt Wines & L. APPLEGAT attended Our regiment remained in billets for training	

Army Form C. 2118.

(24)

WAR DIARY
or
INTELLIGENCE SUMMARY.
(Erase heading not required.)

Instructions regarding War Diaries and Intelligence Summaries are contained in F. S. Regs., Part II. and the Staff Manual respectively. Title pages will be prepared in manuscript.

Hour, Date, Place	Summary of Events and Information	Remarks and references to Appendices
2.6.15	The Regt. 2 wa stay including officers proceeded from trenches at	App IV.
6.6.15 YPRES - WAMERTINGHE & YPRES	YPRES - Draft of 72 men arrived from England. During the period some fighting took place and in the Bde. & supporting heard. The N.S.Y casualties 3 killed 24 wounded. L.O. Keller R.A.M.C. amongst wounded. Complimentary order issued by General Campbell mentioned particularly Bn. D.O.C.	
7.6.15 to STEENBECQUE	Initial 6. Major h. N Stewart offg. Comdg Bttn. Troops proceeded to rail-head and entrained at B.Scribour - Bombs Known by class strain. Capt. L.C Rush & 1st Lancers joined as adjutant. Captain Irons to tempcomd 5th Con Troops. Maps P.E.N Browne Offg Lieutenant Constable yours L.O.Vine. Fox joining. Major C. Broadhurst for Hon. Hanson. Lt.Green. Fox join Comdt. 5th Con Troops. In staff Comdg. 5th Con. Brig. R. Boakle R.G.A. MO W.F. Mecleod Lumins Louis HSH on footpam Comunan Capt. Rawcar MC M. N. said Stones joined. Lt. H.J. Allen & e Cubbie Mc. & O.T.Dykes (M.E.) ouned. Qr. J.E. Biggs R.S.Y. & Tim.RichaRdson N.S.Y. Mc. E. Biggs RSY QTM Richardson NSY. N.C.O.is from 3rd Regts Royals attenu there dept. in many formed. Inspection by G.C.C. Sir John French Kcon.	App. V

've WAR DIARY
INTELLIGENCE SUMMARY.
(Erase heading not required.)

Army Form C. 2118.

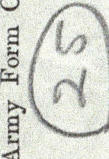

Hour, Date, Place	Summary of Events and Information	Remarks and references to Appendices
27.6.15 to STEENBECQUE	Institute. Division orders established. Swimming knows seven current practices. 2/Lt Jeffrey Raine joined 4/5 W Hampshire Brigade. Regiments at Chocques & Labua. Capt G.B. Brunett and 2/Lt R.B. Queen joined 3/4 N.S.Y.	App IV
16.7.15		
17.7.15 to STEENBECQUE	In Billets. Colonel Ship returned to take over Command. Regiment from division practice for trenches. 14 Brigade Fd. Amb./5.D.1 established. Sgt. H. Jenkins obtained Commission. Regiment now A.R.F.E. with larger	App IV
22.7.15	Area Reconnaissance for duties	
23.7.15 STEENBECQUE	In Billets. Regiment engaged in hoop-scheme division. Regimental and brigade scheme-Swim horns and sports. Pain Lui D. Capt lieu & Co 2/4th 2/5 S.Y. Simon Olson & Lt. Purlestial.	
31.7.15		

3rd Cavalry Brown

121/6807

Котах сринов до:
Vol IX
August 15.

WAR DIARY
or
INTELLIGENCE SUMMARY.
(Erase heading not required.)

Army Form C. 2118.

Hour, Date, Place	Summary of Events and Information	Remarks and references to Appendices
1.8.15. STEENBECQUE	In billets - butter huts.	
4.8.15	Anniversary of Mobilization. Col Glynn. DSO. Capt: A.B. Hutchison. Lt. J.H. Saxton. M.C. & C.T. O'Callaghan. 2. Lt. Fry. RSM. & 2. Lt Op. b. Shakespeare. OR. 1001.	
5.8.15 STEENBECQUE	Battalion paid, under heavy shower, previous to ESTREE BLANCHE SW of AIRE trek on new area. Lim.	App III
6.8.15. ESTREE BLANCHE to WILLERIE	March 6.45 am. for new area and train billets, then had breakfast by Indian Gen. Cav. Lt. Willerie. Regiment under operation orders and forenoon was Lim. Passed troops carrying loot. Regiment came to find party of 150 Reg'rs. 7 Officers. 10 Sergts. 2 Cpls. or Batchman. to go up with the brigade to ARMENTIERES. 2 Lt. M Barkham. in command of party in camp. Remainder of regiment remain in billets. RSM. 1 Reg. K promoted 2/Lt. in 13th Hussars.	
13.8.15. ESTREE BLANCHE	Lim. 7th party to dig at ARMENTIERES proceeded by motor bus. Lt Col Barclow in Command. Maj. C. Stewart. Capt. A.B. Hutchison and 200 O.R.	

WAR DIARY
or
INTELLIGENCE SUMMARY.
(Erase heading not required.)

Army Form C. 2118.

Hour, Date, Place	Summary of Events and Information	Remarks and references to Appendices
15.8.15 ESTREE BLANCHE	Owing to the regiment being employed digging, the remainder of the regiment was occupied in exercise, lectures and grooming. The weather was very fine. Le General Sir Julian Byng KCB gave up command of the Cavalry Corps and Le General Fanshawe took over command. The regiment was visited by Lt Col P. Pabol, Col Wogeyff who has been on a visit to Staff, Lt Capt. M of training. The digging party of "A" Squadron and M Q section returned to commence Squadron training and gun drill. The work done in the trenches was very good.	
1.9.15	The line deep, but the regiment was at HOUPLINES. The remainder of the brigade was at the right. The trenches from EAST from YORKSHIRE POST to run in the regiment sufferance. No casualties, but Lt Regan Sub-altern was killed and one other JR. The weather was fine all the time except to see hours. Huge General Sir Charles Fergusson's God Private Comd. the trenches happen to sent us to work.	Geo/Guy Mqs p.c.c

Sept 19 1915.   North Somerset Yeomanry

I forward herewith Casualty lists up to
Sept 17th for attachment to War Diary.
These will in future be attached at the
end of each month.

Geoffrey Glyn
Lt. Col.

APP. III (3)

BILLETS.

STEENBECQUE — During the summer the regiment was billeted in a close area — good fields and the men in bivouacs: but there was difficulty with water.

ESTREE BLANCHE — The area occupied by the regiment in Aug. included FLECHINELLE. SERNY. LE TIRMAND. LIGNY leaving them 2 not occupied owing to scarcity of water.
At the other places running streams. The coal mines unable even to have baths as the machinery is at work. The accommodation for the officers is moderate and difficulty in finding places for messes. The area was occupied by Indian cavalry and it was left in a bad condition.

Sept. 10 — Brigade asked for information as to the billets for the winter of the regiment in its area. A report was made and room can be found at
ESTREE BLANCHE for H.Q. & section "A" squadron
FLECHINELLE for "B"
SERNY for "C"

Weekly Return of Casualties.

APP. V

Week Ending	Killed		Wounded		Sick		Other Causes
1914.	Officers	Other Ranks	Officers	Other Ranks	Officers	Other Ranks	
6th November							
13th "							
20th "	2	20	2	38			
27th "				1 accidentally		11	1 died of exhaustion, 3 missing (since traced)
4th December						12	
11th "						3	
18th "						6	
25th "						3	
1st January 1915						3	1 died fractured skull
8th "						6	
15th "						5	
22nd "						6	
29th "						8	
5th February						3	
12th "						3	
19th "	1	1		3		1	
26th "						3	
5th March						3	
12th "						3	
19th "						4	
26th "						4	
2nd April						5	
9th "						5	
16th "						7	
23rd "						5	
30th "						7	
7th May		1		1		7	
14th "	3	21	8	79			
21st "						1	2 missing since traced.
28th "						4	
4th June.		3	1	20		8	
	6	46	11	142		136	

Weekly Return of Casualties.

APP. V.

Week ending 1915	Killed Officers	Other Ranks	Wounded Officers	Other Ranks	Sick Officers	Other Ranks	Other Causes
Forward	6	46	11	142		136	
11th June				3		6	
18th "						3	
25th "						6	
2nd July						7	
9th "						11	
16th "					1	10	
23rd "						4	
30th "						8	
6th August						6	
13th "						5	
20th "						3	
27th "						6	
3rd Sept.						1	1 Officer Sick in England
10th "						6	
17th "						5	
	6	46	11	145	1	223	

Analysis from 2 Nov — 17 Sept.

```
  6
 46
 ---
 52      52 K
 11     152 W
145     224 S
---     ---
208     432
  1
223
---
432
```

Officers Killed   6
          Wounded   11
          Sick   1
O.R.   Killed   46
          Wounded   145
          Sick   223
          Total   432

6th Cav.Bde.
3rd Cav.Div.

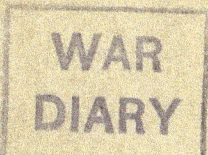

THE NORTH SOMERSET YEOMANRY.

S E P T E M B E R

1 9 1 5

Attached:

Appendix IV.

INTELLIGENCE SUMMARY.

(Erase heading not required.)

Hour, Date, Place	Summary of Events and Information	Remarks and references to Appendices
1.9.15. ESTREE BLANCHE to 19.9.15.	Remainder of outfitting hastily returned from ARMENTIERES on 2—. Draft of 35 men under 2nd Lieut Landseer arrived from England on that date. Further draft of 25 men arrived on 6th. All Squadrons engaged in Squadron training as per syllabus laid down by G.O.C. Two R.f.K. & one R.de. exercise carried out during term period.	APP. IV
20.9.15.	Lt Col. G.C. Glyn appointed to Cavalry Corps for liaison duties. Bde rendez-vous. 6.30 p.m. X Rds B in BELLERY. Marched to BOIS DE DAMES. Strength 22 Officers 385 O.R. excluding Echelond.	

Instructions regarding War Diaries and Intelligence Summaries are contained in F.S. Regs., Part II. and the Staff Manual respectively. Title pages will be prepared in manuscript.

INTELLIGENCE SUMMARY.
(Erase heading not required.)

Hour, Date, Place	Summary of Events and Information	Remarks and references to Appendices
21.9.15 to 24.9.15 BOIS DE DANES	In BOIS DE DANES. Awaiting orders known. Reinforcement to 3 days. Machine gun. Establishment doubled.	On arrival 1 Sept at VERMELLES. a patch of 2 officers (Capt. H.B. MITCHELL 2nd Lieut. C.T.O'CALLAGHAN)
25.9.15.	B.de marched 8.30 a.m. to VAUDRICOURT & thence via NOEUX LES MINES to VERMELLES STATION. arrival about 12.	1/13 has been sent to reinnoitre the front & discover active position.
26.9.15.	Regiment standing to all day. 3rd Dragoons (ment). & 1st Royals sent about 2 p.m. to occupy captured line 1 German trenches on immediate right & left from BETHUNE LENS Rd. They however being torn ret. orders to advance to occupy LOOS.	from infantry, holding our trenches. 1 State of trenches. Nice hiles made apparent but want of hills to c + height back very good information.
2.p.m.		
5.30.p.m.	Regiment ret. orders to occupy line 1 captured German trenches from LOOS ROAD REDOUBT. See list. w3.	2 times wounded hostile cavalry. Patrol returned about 5 p.m.

INTELLIGENCE SUMMARY.

(Erase heading not required.)

Hour, Date, Place	Summary of Events and Information	Remarks and references to Appendices
26.9.15. LOOS.	to NORTH LOOS AVENUE exclusive. Men line was formed the already held by the 2nd Grenadier Gds., & after considerable difficulty in getting orders, Regiment was directed & proceed to LOOS, to reinforce. Remainder of Bn. arrived there about 2 a.m. on 27 & took up a line from post 58 to between 72 & 27. Ref sheet 36C. N.W.3 & P.9.1. 1:10000. 1st R.D's on our right. 3rd Dragoon Guards holding SE outskirts of town & joining up 8th Cavalry Bde. on our left. 2nd Grenadier Gds.	
27. a.m. p.m.	Improving quickly. Spent in improving trenches. Guards Brigade on our left attacked due E about 4.30. Heavy shelling during afternoon. Shells getting chiefly	2 prisoners captured with telephone & wife next hiding in cellar.

Forms/C. 2118/10

(9 29 6) W 4141—463 100,000 9/14 H W V

INTELLIGENCE SUMMARY.
(Erase heading not required.)

Instructions regarding War Diaries and Intelligence Summaries are contained in F.S. Regs., Part II. and the Staff Manual respectively. Title pages will be prepared in manuscript.

Hour, Date, Place	Summary of Events and Information	Remarks and references to Appendices
LOOS. 27.9.15	On road behind our French trenches. Found gas shells & smoke helmets in use. Regt. disposed as follows. "B" squadron in reserve. "C" squadron on left. 1 troop on "D" Scots Guards. "A" squadron on right of "C". 2 troops "C" squadron in cellars. As trenches overcrowded – Machine gun in a strong supporting about 2 Guards Bde. One canadian were wounded. Sufficient 10 other ranks – light. Knit. Trenches informed.	
28.9.15	Rather whole. Spasmodic shelling recommenced during afternoon. Very heavy Artillery	

INTELLIGENCE SUMMARY.
(Erase heading not required.)

Hour, Date, Place	Summary of Events and Information	Remarks and references to Appendices
28.9.15. LOOS.	bombardment chiefly on our left + in centre plain - no casualties - Regiment relieved about 11 p.m. by 1st Northants Regt. + marched back to MARINGARBE.	reported wire cut
29.9.15. Bois de Dames.	Bde marched back to Bois de DAMES. in bivouac	
30.9.15. "	Regiment resting - troops if required.	

APPENDIX IV.

Strength APP IV

A draft of 35 men joined from England. Their training is better than some that came before.

5. A draft of 25 men and 25 horses joined, both good material.

2/Lt Vandeleur joined from Rouen in the place of Lt. Cowie struck off and sent to a Mortar Company.

[signature]
Lt Col

OCG/7520/121

8th Cavalry Bde.

N# Somme Day.

Oct 20

III 5

Army Form C. 2118.

WAR DIARY
or
INTELLIGENCE SUMMARY.
(Erase heading not required.)

Instructions regarding War Diaries and Intelligence Summaries are contained in F.S. Regs., Part II. and the Staff Manual respectively. Title pages will be prepared in manuscript.

Hour, Date, Place		Summary of Events and Information	Remarks and references to Appendices
1-10-15	BOIS de DAMES	Regiment still in the wood, in a state of readiness.	
2- " -	— " —	ditto. Received orders to be ready to move troops at short notice.	
3-10-15	BOIS de DAMES FERFAY.	Marched from the BOIS de DAMES at about 3 pm and got into temporary billets at FERFAY about 6 pm.	
4-10-15 to 8-10-15	FERFAY.	General clean up, and checking of Arms, Saddlery, and Equipment.	
9-10-15	FERFAY	Inspection of Regiment in Marching Order by C.O.	
11-10-15	— " —	Regt practised a dismounted attack.	
12-10-15 to 16-10-15	— " —	Regt and Squadron Training. Regt & Sqn Recomn movings courses of Bombing under instruction of R.E. Officer.	
18-10-15	FERFAY	Had a good day at Regimental Drill.	
19-10-15	LAIRES	Brigade moved Billets 10½ in Westerly direction, the Regt and 1st Royal Dgns being billeted in LAIRES.	
20-10-15	— " —	Orders to move to permanent billets at AMETTES tomorrow	

Army Form C. 2118.

WAR DIARY
or
INTELLIGENCE SUMMARY.
(Erase heading not required.)

Instructions regarding War Diaries and Intelligence Summaries are contained in F. S. Regs., Part II. and the Staff Manual respectively. Title pages will be prepared in manuscript.

Hour, Date, Place	Summary of Events and Information	Remarks and references to Appendices
21-10-15 AMETTES.	Arrived in permanent billeting area. A. B. & H⁰Q⁵ at AMETTES. C and Machine Gun NEDON.	
22-10-15 AMETTES	Billets of C and Machine Gun found not satisfactory	
23-10-15 AMETTES	C Squadron moved billets to AUCHY au BOIS and Machine Gun Section to TATINGLOUX.	
24-10-15 to 28-10-15 AMETTES	Settling into Billets. Repairing stables, Barns, Roads. etc.	
29-10-15 AMETTES	Marching Order Inspection and Route march for Regt by C.O	
30-31-10-15 AMETTES	Squadron Training	

Forms/C. 2118/10

3rd Cavalry Division

nôs souvenirs Geo.

nov. V 1915
vol. VII

17449
/31

WAR DIARY — NORTH SOMERSET YEOMANRY

INTELLIGENCE SUMMARY.

(Erase heading not required.)

Army Form C. 2118

Hour, Date, Place	Summary of Events and Information	Remarks and references to Appendices
1-XI to 8th XI 1915. AMETTES.	Improving winter billets, and Squadron Training.	
9-XI-15 AMETTES.	Two NCOs, 3 NCOs & 75 men digging party to OUDERDOM. Major Dennis in charge of Res. Party.	
10 to 16-XI-15 —"—	Improving Billets, and training when possible, not able to do much, digging party being away.	
17-XI-15 On the march.	Brigade moved into new billeting area. The Regt. parated at 9 am and moved via LAIRES – LUGY – FRUGES – CREQUY – ROYON to HESMOND. Head Quarters and A Squadron billets at HESMOND, B. C and machine Gun Section at LEBIEZ. Roads covered with snow, very bad travelling.	
18-XI-15 HESMOND	Settling into billets. Hard frost, roads very slippery, impossible for horses not roughed.	
19-IX-15 —"—		

Army Form C. 2118

WAR DIARY
or
INTELLIGENCE SUMMARY.
(Erase heading not required.)

Instructions regarding War Diaries and Intelligence Summaries are contained in F. S. Regs., Part II. and the Staff Manual respectively. Title pages will be prepared in manuscript.

Hour, Date, Place	Summary of Events and Information	Remarks and references to Appendices
20.XI.15 HESMOND	Receives draft of 2 th men and 23 horses. Improving billets.	
21 "	Improving billets.	
22 "	Digging party returned, and isolated on account of scabies.	
23-30th XI.15 "	Improving billets and individual training.	

M.R. Backhouse Lieut. Colonel.

M. NORTH SOMERSET YEOMANRY.

N⟨o⟩ Somervail Geo.
Dec 1915.
Vol. VIII

6/ 3rd Cav. Div

Army Form C. 2118.

WAR DIARY
or
INTELLIGENCE SUMMARY.
(Erase heading not required.)

Hour, Date, Place	Summary of Events and Information	Remarks and references to Appendices
1915. 1 – 7TH DECEMBER HESMOND.	Usual winter routine was carried on during the month, but under considerable difficulties owing to shortage in men and the fact that A Squadron was segregated on account of an outbreak of measles. A number of subaltern officers were sent up to the trenches for instruction and experience in the trenches with infantry battalions	

VIII

N⁰5 Somervell Sec.
Date 1915.
Vol.

6/3rd Cav. Div.

NORTH SOMERSET YEOMANRY

Army Form C. 2118.

WAR DIARY
or
INTELLIGENCE SUMMARY.
(Erase heading not required.)

Instructions regarding War Diaries and Intelligence Summaries are contained in F. S. Regs., Part II. and the Staff Manual respectively. Title pages will be prepared in manuscript.

Hour, Date, Place	Summary of Events and Information	Remarks and references to Appendices
1915. 1—7th December HESMOND.	Usual winter routine was carried on during the month, but under considerable difficulties owing to shortage in men and the fact that a squadron was segregated on account of an outbreak of measles. A number of subaltern officers were sent up to the trenches for instruction and experience in the trenches with infantry battalions.	

NORTH SOMERSET YEOMANRY

Army Form C. 2118.

WAR DIARY
or
INTELLIGENCE SUMMARY.
(Erase heading not required.)

Instructions regarding War Diaries and Intelligence Summaries are contained in F.S. Regs., Part II. and the Staff Manual respectively. Title pages will be prepared in manuscript.

Hour, Date, Place	Summary of Events and Information	Remarks and references to Appendices
1915. DECEMBER. HESMOND.	The instruction of the Regimental Bombers under 2 Lieut J.G. Biggs was carried on with great activity and satisfactory results. A digging party under the command of Captain A. Gordon, composed of 3 Officers 89 N.C.Os and men proceeded to LYNDE on the 10th and 13th for digging operations renewing these until they were withdrawn on Christmas Eve.	

NORTH SOMERSET YEOMANRY.

Army Form C. 2118.

WAR DIARY
or
INTELLIGENCE SUMMARY.
(Erase heading not required.)

Instructions regarding War Diaries and Intelligence Summaries are contained in F. S. Regs., Part II. and the Staff Manual respectively. Title pages will be prepared in manuscript.

Hour, Date, Place	Summary of Events and Information	Remarks and references to Appendices
1915 DECEMBER. HESMOND.	Various officers attended French mortar and dugout courses.	
26th December	The Dismounted Company was mobilised so from 6 p.m. 26th December. Details of which will appear in the January diary. Weather during the month – Wet and Mild. Billeting area on the whole more too satisfactory, but with the	

NORTH SOMERSET YEOMANRY.

Army Form C. 2118.

WAR DIARY
or
INTELLIGENCE SUMMARY.

(Erase heading not required.)

Instructions regarding War Diaries and Intelligence
Summaries are contained in F.S. Regs., Part II.
and the Staff Manual respectively. Title pages
will be prepared in manuscript.

Hour, Date, Place	Summary of Events and Information	Remarks and references to Appendices
1915 DECEMBER HESMOND.	ception of the outbreak of measles, the health of the Regiment was extraordinarily good.	

M.R. Barkhurst
Lieut Colonel
Commanding, North Somerset Yeomanry

Hort. Soc. of Geo.
Jan. 1916.
Vol IX

3rd Copy

WAR DIARY or INTELLIGENCE SUMMARY

Army Form C. 2118

Place	Date Jan 1916	Hour	Summary of Events and Information	Remarks and references to Appendices
HESMOND	1-1-16		The 6th Dismounted Battalion ordered to entrain at MARESQUEL on the 3rd inst.	
-"-	2nd		Final inspection of H.Q.Y. Company. Transport proceed to MARESQUEL STN	
-"-	3rd		The 6th Dis Batt. entrained at MARESQUEL at 9am to proceed to BETHUNE for duty in front line. Strength 9 officers 300 O.R. N.S.Y.Coy. 2 Offrs. 26 O.R. 12 Drivers. Strength 9 Offrs. M.E. Sections, 2 Offrs 2 Sgts. 26 O.R. 12 Drivers. Transport 12 Drivers. Attached to Batt. Hd Qrs 4 Chicken Runs, 1 chewing Anvil.	
-"-	4 to 11th		Weather fine. Men of Royals & 3rd D.G.s attached for grooming owing to shortage of men.	
-"-	12th		Major H. BARNER-HAHLO, 2 Lt. E.A. GREEN and 100 other ranks joined from England as Demounted Squadron.	
-"-	13th		Men of Royals & 3 D.G. sent back to own Regts.	
14 to 28			Exercise and Grooming, nothing of importance to note.	
-"-	29th		H.Q. of N.S.Y. proceed to take over H.Q. of 6th Dis Battalion in relief of 1st Royals.	

Army Form C. 2118

WAR DIARY
or
INTELLIGENCE SUMMARY
(Erase heading not required.)

Instructions regarding War Diaries and Intelligence Summaries are contained in F.S. Regs., Part II. and the Staff Manual respectively. Title Pages will be prepared in manuscript.

Place	Date	Hour	Summary of Events and Information	Remarks and references to Appendices
HESMOND	30th 31st		Nothing of importance. Exercise & Grooming being all that could be done during absence of Div. Coy.	

Wm Stewart K. Major
for O.C. North Somerset Yeomanry

Army Form C. 2118

WAR DIARY
INTELLIGENCE SUMMARY
(Erase heading not required.)

Instructions regarding War Diaries and Intelligence Summaries are contained in F. S. Regs. Part II. and the Staff Manual respectively. Title Pages will be prepared in manuscript.

Place	Date	Hour	Summary of Events and Information	Remarks and references to Appendices
HESMOND	Feb 1-10 1916		Dismounted Company still away. Exercise & Grooming.	
—"—	11th		6th Battn. 1st Bn. 6th Battalion detrained at MARESQUEL at about 8.30 p.m. Casualties of Regt. Company during time away. Killed 3 O.R. Died of wounds 2 O.R. Wounded 1 Officer (2/Lt WHISH) and 14 O.R.	
—"—	12th–29th		Regt. in billets. Work carried out, Troop and Squadron Training.	

M Mackenzie
Lieut. Colonel
Commanding 1st ... ...

Army Form C. 2118.

WAR DIARY
INTELLIGENCE SUMMARY.
(Erase heading not required.)

ho I

Instructions regarding War Diaries and Intelligence Summaries are contained in F.S. Regs., Part II. and the Staff Manual respectively. Title pages will be prepared in manuscript.

Hour, Date, Place 1916.	Summary of Events and Information	Remarks and references to Appendices
HESMOND. March 1st	2 Officers (2/Lt M.H. TISDALL and 2/Lt F.B. RATCLIFFE) 67 other ranks, 95 horses, 6 timbered G.S. wagons and 2 bicycles, struck off the strength and attached to 6th Machine Gun Squadron.	
" 1 - 9th	Troop & Squadron Training.	
" 10th	Inspection of Regt. in Marching Order by G.O.C. 6th Cavalry Brigade.	
" 11th - 14th	Squadron Training.	
" 15th	Regt Route March	
" 16 - 17th	Squadron Training	
" 18th	Tactical tour for C.O. and 2nd in Command by G.O.C. 6th Cav. Bde.	
" 19 - 26th	Sqn Training	
" 27 - 29th	Brigade Route March.	
" 30 - 31st	Regimental Training.	

WAR DIARY

INTELLIGENCE SUMMARY.

Army Form C. 2118.

Hour, Date, Place	Summary of Events and Information	Remarks and references to Appendices
April 1916 HESMOND. 1-18th	Squadron Training. Afternoon instruction in Bayonet fighting, bombing, Pioneering, Sniping & Hotchkiss Gun by Officers and N.C.Os. who have been through the 3rd Cavalry Division Training School.	
—"— 19	Inspection of Regt. by G.O.C. 3rd Cav. Divn.	
—"— 20-30th	Squadron Training and instruction of Specialists as above.	

WAR DIARY 1/1st Somerset Yeomanry Army Form C. 2118
or
INTELLIGENCE SUMMARY
(Erase heading not required.)

Instructions regarding War Diaries and Intelligence Summaries are contained in F.S. Regs., Part II. and the Staff Manual respectively. Title Pages will be prepared in manuscript.

Vol 13

Place	Date 1916	Hour	Summary of Events and Information	Remarks and references to Appendices
HESMOND PARIS-PLAGE	1st May		The Regiment moved by march route to camp at PARIS-PLAGE. Camp near the sea and LE TOUQUET Golf Links. Camp designated STONEHAM CAMP.	
STONEHAM CAMP	2-6		Regt Drill on the sands, practice of close formation, and Infantry attacks formation during morning, afternoon work, musketry, diamond's stick through nose's and spiricheks.	
-"-	7		Church Parade service by the Rev J.S. Estes Chaplain to 8th Cav Bde.	
-"-	8-13		Regt Drill on sands and practice of attack tactic. Afternoon work as in previous week.	
-"-	14		Memorial Service for Officers NCO's & men, killed on 13th May 1915.	
-"-	15		Reveille Troops and Echelon A marched to Divisional Training Area at ST RIQUIER near ABBEVILLE. Dismounted Squadron and Echelon B to permanent billets.	
ST.RIQUIER	16-20		Divisional Training	
-"-	21		March back to permanent billets.	
HESMOND	22-31		Horses doing very little work. Staff rides for Young Officers & NCO's	

M Kirkwood Lieut Colonel
Commanding 1/1st Somerset Yeomanry

Army Form C. 2118.

WAR DIARY work front Germany
or
INTELLIGENCE SUMMARY.

(Erase heading not required.)

Instructions regarding War Diaries and Intelligence Summaries are contained in F.S. Regs., Part II. and the Staff Manual respectively. Title pages will be prepared in manuscript.

Vol 16

Hour, Date, Place	Summary of Events and Information	Remarks and references to Appendices
HESMOND. 1 — 23 June 1916	Regt. and Squadron Training. Nothing special to note.	
" — 24th "	Regt. paraded at 6 pm to march to Bois Rudezones. Strength, Fighting Troops 419 all ranks 427 horses. Echelon A 64 men 99 horses. Echelon B 35 men 45 horses. Bivouacked in junction 94 alternate. The Bde marched at 8.30 pm via HESDIN and billeted in FROYELLES district.	
On the march 25th	Left FROYELLES 8 pm via DOMART en PONTHIEU and billeted in PERNOIS. (SOMME)	
" 26th	Left PERNOIS 8 pm via VIGNACOURT — BERTANGLES — QUERRIEU and reached BONNAY in the Cavalry Concentration Area at 4.15 am on 27th. Rain fell almost the whole of the march.	
BONNAY 27th to 30th	Horses picketed in ninety ground now had to get cover from Aeroplane Prowlers. Weather very unsettled. Fighting Troops issued with Steel Helmets on 29th. Everything ready for a forward move which is expected to take place on the 1st July 1916.	

30/6/16

M Barthorp?
Lieut Colonel
Commanding North Somerset Yeo.

Sheet 1

Army Form C. 2118.

WAR DIARY North Somerset Yeomanry

or

INTELLIGENCE SUMMARY.

(Erase heading not required.)

Instructions regarding War Diaries and Intelligence Summaries are contained in F. S. Regs., Part II. and the Staff Manual respectively. Title pages will be prepared in manuscript.

Hour, Date, Place 1916	Summary of Events and Information	Remarks and references to Appendices
BONNAY. July 1st 2nd 3rd	Regiment "standing to" at BONNAY. Orders received at 10 p.m. on evening of 3rd to move, the Brigade to be clear of the area by 6 a.m. on the 4th.	
" " 4th	The Bde paraded at 5.15 am and marched via DAOURS – AMIENS – AILLY-SUR-SOMME – HANGEST-SUR-SOMME to billets are around AIRAINES. N.S.Y. billeted in ALLERY, arrived in billets at 4.30 p.m.	
ALLERY " 5th	2Lt FEARNLEY and 58 OR of Dismounted Squadron proceeded by train to MERICOURT to work under orders of 15th Corps.	
" " 6th 7th	Regiment in billets, nothing of importance to record.	
" " 8th	The Bde assembled at 2.15 p.m. and marched via AILLY SUR SOMME AMIENS to CORBIE arriving in Bivouac at about 2.30 am 9th.	
CORBIE " 9th	Reinforcements of 12 OR received from Base. 20 OR of dismounted squadron details for duty with N.6 R.E. Park MERICOURT. Bivouac not being satisfactory the Bde moved to Bivouac at VAUX-SUR-SOMME arriving there at 6.15 p.m.	
VAUX SUR SOMME " 10–13	Nothing of importance to record.	
" " 14–18	A draft of 3 OR and 6 riding horses arrived on the 14th, and 4 OR and 9 riding horses on the 15th from the Base.	
" " 19th	Bde moved to billeting area at LA NEUVILLE. 2Lt TAYLOR and 53 OR. sent to relieve the party at MERICOURT which left the Regt on the 5th. The relieved party rejoined the Regt on arrival at LA NEUVILLE.	
LA NEUVILLE " 20th 24th	Casualties during this time of duty 1 OR died of wounds 4 OR wounded. Nothing of importance to record.	

(9 29 6) W 4141—463 100,000 9/14 H W V Forms/C. 2118/10

WAR DIARY North Somerset Yeomany Sect 2 Army Form C. 2118.
or
INTELLIGENCE SUMMARY.
(Erase heading not required.)

Hour, Date, Place	Summary of Events and Information	Remarks and references to Appendices
LA NEUVILLE July 25th 1916	2 Officers and 96 O.R. sent mounted to BECOURT to work under the orders of 13th Corps, sufficient men being sent to bring back Kiw Horses to bivouac.	
" 26th	2/Lt TAYLOR's party returned from MERICOURT. No casualties.	
" 27th	A further party sent to BECOURT of 2 Officers and 90 O.R. to work under orders of 13th Corps	
" 28th	Major G. LUBBOCK, 1 Officer and 6 riding horses joined from Base. Nothing of importance to record.	
" 29-30	All working parties recalled, as Brigade is ordered to move westwards on the 1st of August. Horses sent to guard party from BECOURT, the 20 O.R. doing duty with 6th R.E. Park returning by Motor Transport. No casualties.	
" 31st		

M Backhouse
Lt Colonel N.S.Y.

Sheet I. 1/1 [?] Armd Amroc[?] Germany Army Form C. 2118
August 1916.

WAR DIARY
or
INTELLIGENCE SUMMARY
(Erase heading not required.)

Instructions regarding War Diaries and Intelligence Summaries are contained in F.S. Regs., Part II. and the Staff Manual respectively. Title Pages will be prepared in manuscript.

Place	Date 1916	Hour	Summary of Events and Information	Remarks and references to Appendices
LA NEUVILLE	1-Aug	6 am	The Regt (less Dismounted Squadron) moved, as part of the 6th Cav Bde. via by march route DADURS - AMIENS - LONGPRE - AILLY sur SOMME - PICQUIGNY, to SOUES, arriving in bivouac at about 3 pm.	
SOUES	2 "	5 am	March continued via AIRAINES - SOREL - LIERCOURT - PONT REMY - BUIGNY L'ABBÉ - VAUCHELLES to NEUF-MOULIN arriving in bivouac about 2.30 pm. The Dismounted Squadron [?] arriving the evening having moved from LA NEUVILLE by train to CANDAS.	
NEUF-MOULIN	3 "		Regiment in bivouac at NEUF-MOULIN. The G.O.C 3rd Cavalry Division held a conference with all officers of the Division down to, and including, Squadron Leaders, on the subject of Training.	
NEUF-MOULIN	4 "	5 am	March continued via DOMVAST - MARCHEVILLE - CRECY - LIGESCOURT to MAINTENAY arriving in bivouac about 11 am. The Dismounted Squadron moved by 'bus' from NEUF-MOULIN direct to permanent billets at HESMOND.	
MAINTENAY	5 "	7.35 am	March continued via BUIRE le SEC - CAMPAGNE les HESDIN - BEAURAINVILLE to permanent billets at HESMOND - LEBIEZ arriving at about 11 am. Regt Head Quarters and A Squadron at HESMOND, B and C Squadrons at LEBIEZ.	
HESMOND	6-10		Regt settling down into billets. Inspection of Bit Saddlery and Horses. 3 drafts on the 8th met for duty with the 2/1st Inf Division.	
ROYON	11		Regt Head Quarters moved from HESMOND to ROYON taking over the billets previously occupied by the Hd Qrs 6th Cavalry Brigade, move completed by 12 noon.	
-"-	12		Nothing of importance to report	
-"-	13		Divisional Working Party left by train for duty under the 2nd Corps. Capt W. Stir [?] Wills in charge of Bde Party. Regt Party : 2 Lieut E.A. HUTCHINGS and 59 other ranks.	
-"-	14		Squadron Training. Recruits from 6/15 am to 9 am. Dismounted training from 2.30 to 3.30 pm.	

1875. Wt. W593/826 1.000.000 4/15 J.B.C. & A. A.D.S.S./Forms/C. 2118.

Sheet 2.

WAR DIARY

INTELLIGENCE SUMMARY

Army Form C. 2118

1/4th Somerset Yeomanry   August 1916.

Place	Date 1916 August	Hour	Summary of Events and Information	Remarks and references to Appendices
ROYON	15-19		Squadron Training. Permitted work from 6-15 am until 9 am. Diamonds Training 2.30 pm until 3.30 pm. Specialist classes in Bombing, Hotchkiss Rifle, Sniping, Signalling, & Bayonet fighting.	Mr
-"-	20	10am	Church Parade at ROYON. Band under Sgt Costello played the hymns during the service.	Mr
-"-	20		The 3 Snipers with 21st Division relieved by 3 others.	Mr
-"-	21		Squadron Training	Mr
-"-	22		Squadron Training. Lecture by the Rev Canon Hannay (Geo. A. Birmingham) on "Irish Humour".	Mr
-"-	23		Anticipated rumours that Division will probably move on 25th inst.	Mr
-"-	24		Probable move cancelled.	Mr
-"-	25.26.27		Nothing of importance to report.	Mr
-"-	28-31		Squadron Training. Working party under 2nd Corps being relieved in two parties, 1st party 1 Offr and 30 men on 31st August, 2nd party Capt O.W Phipps & 29 men on the 1st September.	Mr

Jn Bartholo.
Lieut. Colonel
Commanding 2/4 Somerset Yeomanry

6 Cav./3

Vol 17

WAR DIARY.

NORTH SOMERSET YEOMANRY.

1st to 30th SEPTEMBER 1916.

VOL. I3.

Army Form C. 2118.

WAR DIARY
INTELLIGENCE SUMMARY

North Annual Germany

(Erase heading not required.)

Instructions regarding War Diaries and Intelligence Summaries are contained in F. S. Regs., Part II. and the Staff Manual respectively. Title pages will be prepared in manuscript.

Hour, Date, Place		Summary of Events and Information	Remarks and references to Appendices
1·IX·16	ROYON.	In billets. Inspection of Regimental Transport by the Commanding Officer. Training in Hotchkiss, signalling and Bombing classes.	[sig]
2·IX·16.	ROYON.	In billets. Exercise, saddlery and kit inspection.	[sig]
3·IX·16.	"	In billets. Regiment attended Divine Service.	[sig]
4·IX·16	"	" Training in Hotchkiss, signalling and Bombing classes.	[sig]
5·IX·16	"	" The Regiment took part in a scheme with the 3rd Dragoon Guards. 2nd Lieut J.V.C. Rice and 3 Other Ranks (snipers) proceeded to the 51st Division.	[sig]
6·IX·16	"	" Transport Inspection by the G.O.C., 6th Cavalry Brigade and the D.G., A.S.C., 3rd Cavalry Division. Dismounted party and arms regtn Regiment. Training in Hotchkiss, signalling and Bombing classes.	[sig]
7·IX·16	"	"	[sig]
8·IX·16.	"	"	[sig]
9·IX·16	"	" Exercise, saddlery and kit inspections.	[sig]

Army Form C. 2118.

WAR DIARY
or
INTELLIGENCE SUMMARY.
(Erase heading not required.)

North Irish Horse

Instructions regarding War Diaries and Intelligence Summaries are contained in F.S. Regs., Part II. and the Staff Manual respectively. Title pages will be prepared in manuscript.

Hour, Date, Place		Summary of Events and Information	Remarks and references to Appendices
10.IX.1916	ROYON.	In billets.	The Regiment paraded at 8.30 A.M. and proceeded to SAULCHOY via BEAURAINVILLE arriving at 12 noon. Horses picketed and men bivouaced in a park near the village.	[signed]
11.IX.1916	SAULCHOY.	In bivouac.	The Regiment marched at noon to a new billeting area and bivouaced at NEUILLY L'HOPITAL (Route:- LE PETIT CHEMIN, CRECY-EN-PONTHIEU, BOIS DE CRECY, LA MOTTE BULEUX.) arrived at 6 p.m. and bivouaced in fields on the outskirts of the village.	[signed]
12.IX.1916	NEUILLY L'HOPITAL.	In bivouac.	The Regiment marched at 11 AM to LA CHAUSSÉE via VAUCHELLES — PONT REMY — FLIXECOURT. arriving at 5 p.m. and bivouaced in fields close to village.	[signed]
13.IX.1916	LA CHAUSSÉE	In bivouac.		[signed]

Army Form C. 2118.

WAR DIARY
or
INTELLIGENCE SUMMARY. North Somerset Yeomanry.
(Erase heading not required.)

Hour, Date, Place		Summary of Events and Information	Remarks and references to Appendices
14.IX.1916. LA CHAUSSEE.	In bivouac.	The Regiment marched to BUSSY-LES-DAOURS. at 6.45 A.M. via AMIENS.	[initials]
15.IX.1916. BUSSY-LES-DAOURS.	"	The Regiment paraded at 9.15 A.M. marched to BONNAY via O of DAOURS. fixed bivouac BONNAY — LA NEUVILLE Road, S.E. of BONNAY. DAOURS — LA NEUVILLE Road, S.E. of still 60 leading to O of BONNAY. The Brigade arrived BONNAY 10 A.M. and bivouacked. Stood to at ½ hour notice.	[initials]
16.IX.1916. BONNAY.	"	Stood to at ½ hour notice from 9 A.M.	[initials]
17.IX.1916. BONNAY.	"	The Regiment marched at 9 A.M. to PONT NOYELLES arrived 9.15 A.M. Division concentrated at PONT NOYELLES. State of readiness of Brigade to move at ½ hour notice.	[initials]
18.IX.1916. BONNAY.	"		[initials]

Army Form C. 2118.

WAR DIARY
or
INTELLIGENCE SUMMARY.
(Erase heading not required.)

Instructions regarding War Diaries and Intelligence Summaries are contained in F.S. Regs., Part II. and the Staff Manual respectively. Title pages will be prepared in manuscript.

Hour, Date, Place		Summary of Events and Information	Remarks and references to Appendices
19.IX.1916	PONT NOYELLES	In bivouac. Squadrons exercised and grazed.	[initials]
20.IX.1916	PONT NOYELLES	" Squadrons exercised and grazed.	[initials]
21.IX.1916	PONT NOYELLES	" Squadrons exercised and grazed.	[initials]
22.IX.1916	PONT NOYELLES	" The Regiment marched to SOUES via LA MOTTE, CAMON, AMIENS, PICQUIGNY, + arrived at SOUES at 6 p.m. + bivouacked in the fields.	[initials]
23.IX.1916	SOUES	" The Regiment marched to BEALCOURT via FLIXECOURT — cross to N. bank of River. — HALTE. (N of ST OUEN.) — W end of DOMART-en-PONTHIEU. arrived about 4.30 p.m. and bivouacked.	[initials]
24.IX.1916	BEALCOURT	" Marched at 5.45 A.M. to SAULCHOY via LE PONCHEL — LABROYE arrived SAULCHOY about 3 p.m. and bivouacked.	[initials]

Army Form C. 2118.

WAR DIARY
or
INTELLIGENCE SUMMARY.

North Somerset Yeomanry.

(Erase heading not required.)

Instructions regarding War Diaries and Intelligence Summaries are contained in F.S. Regs., Part II. and the Staff Manual respectively. Title pages will be prepared in manuscript.

Hour, Date, Place		Summary of Events and Information	Remarks and references to Appendices
25.IX.1916	SAULCHOY	In bivouac. Squadrons exercised, Bit and Saddlery Inspections	[initials]
26.IX.1916	SAULCHOY	" Squadrons exercised	[initials]
27.IX.1916	SAULCHOY	" Squadrons exercised	[initials]
28.IX.1916	SAULCHOY	" "	[initials]
29.IX.1916	SAULCHOY	" Regiment marched at 8.45am to a new billeting area at MERLIMONT-CUCQ-MERLIMONT PLAGE. Arrived about 12 noon. "A" & "B" Squadrons billeted at MERLIMONT. "C" Squadron billeted at CUCQ. Regt Headquarters - MERLIMONT PLAGE.	[initials]
30.IX.1916	MERLIMONT PLAGE.	In billets. Squadron training on the sands. Training of stretcher bearers, gun teams and signallers. Commands classes.	[initials]

F. Buckhouse Lt. Col.
Commanding North Somerset Yeomanry.

Vol 18

WAR DIARY.

NORTH SOMERSET YEOMANRY.

1st to 31st OCTOBER 1916.

VOL. 24.

WAR DIARY

INTELLIGENCE SUMMARY. NORTH SOMERSET YEOMANRY.

Army Form C. 2118.

1st to 31st OCTOBER 1916.

Place	Date	Hour	Summary of Events and Information	Remarks and references to Appendices
MERIMONT PLAGE	1.10.16		In billets. Regiment attended Divine Service.	y.R
"	2.10.16		In billets. Squadron Training. Training of Hotchkiss Gun Teams, Signallers and Corporals classes. 2/Lieut. T.H. Hurst & 56 O.R. dismounted party, proceeded to HESDIN by M.T. Lorries and entrained for BELLE EGLISSE, W. of ACHEUX for attachment to 2nd Corps.	y.R
"	3.10.16		In billets. Squadron exercises. Bayonet fighting & Corporals class.	y.R
"	4.10.16		In billets. Squadron drill on sands. Firing of Hotchkiss guns.	y.R
"	5.10.16		In billets. Regimental Drill on sands. Inspection of Regimental Transport by Camp Officer. Bayonet fighting. Corporals class.	y.R
"	6.10.16		In billets. Squadron training. Hotchkiss Gun, Signalling & Corporals classes.	y.R

Army Form C. 2118

WAR DIARY
or
INTELLIGENCE SUMMARY.
(Erase heading not required.)

Instructions regarding War Diaries and Intelligence Summaries are contained in F. S. Regs., Part II. and the Staff Manual respectively. Title pages will be prepared in manuscript.

Place	Date	Hour	Summary of Events and Information	Remarks and references to Appendices
MERLIMONT PLAGE	7.10.16		In billets. G.O.C. 6th Cavalry Bde. inspects the horses of the Regiment at MERLIMONT and C.U.C.Q. Saddlery & Kit inspections	Y.D.
"	8.10.16		In billets. Regiment attended Divine Service at C.U.C.Q.	Y.D.
"	9.10.16		In billets. G.O.C. 6th Cavalry Bde. inspected "C" Sqdn. in marching order at C.U.C.Q. "A" & "B" Squadrons inspected in marching order by C.O. at MERLIMONT. Signallers & Scouts classed	Y.D.
"	10.10.16		In billets. Regimental Drill in ernes. Inspection of Signallers by Bde. Signal Officer. Firing of Hotchkiss Guns. Capt. H.A. Kroenen D.S.O. 13th Hussars att'd. N.S.Y. proceeds to 2nd Corps to take command of 3rd Division Dismounted party.	Y.D.
"	11.10.16		In billets. Squadron Training. Dummy Shooting. Learning Hotchkiss Gun Gears.	Y.D.
"	12.10.16		In billets. "B" Sqdn. took part in Brigade Scheme. "A" & "C" Sqns. Squadron Training. Corporals Class. Bayonet fighting.	Y.D.

Army Form C. 2118.

WAR DIARY
or
INTELLIGENCE SUMMARY.

(Erase heading not required.)

Instructions regarding War Diaries and Intelligence Summaries are contained in F.S. Regs., Part II. and the Staff Manual respectively. Title pages will be prepared in manuscript.

Place	Date	Hour	Summary of Events and Information	Remarks and references to Appendices
MERLIMONT PLAGE	13.10.16		2nd Lill'd R. Regimental Drill in sands, Infantry attack practices - Cyclists class, Signalling & Bayonet fighting.	yrd
"	14.10.16		2nd Lill'd R. Squadrons exercises. Saddling Kit inspection.	yrd
"	15.10.16		2nd Lill'd R. Regiment attended Divine Service at MERLIMONT PLAGE.	yrd
"	16.10.16		2nd Lill'd R. Regimental Drill in sands - Signalling, Hotchkiss Gun & Cyclists classes. Major C.H. Delamere 31st Lancers joined & took over duties 2nd in command N.S.H.	yrd
"	17.10.16		2nd Lill'd R. Squadron training. Inspection of Hotchkiss Guns by C.O. Signalling & Cyclists classes.	yrd
"	18.10.16		2nd Lill'd R. Squadrons exercises.	yrd
"	19.10.16		2nd Lill'd R. Regimental Drill - Mounted attack on Infantry - Signalling & Cyclists classes.	yrd

WAR DIARY
or
INTELLIGENCE SUMMARY.

Army Form C. 2118.

Place	Date	Hour	Summary of Events and Information	Remarks and references to Appendices
MERLIMONT PLAGE	20.10.16		In billets. Squadron training. Dummy shooting. Instruction of Subaltern Officers under 2nd in command. Signalling & rifle classes. Lieut. W.G. Salmon & 70 O.R. proceed to BOUZINCOURT attached to 2nd Corps in relief of dismounted party of 83 O.R. under Lt. T.H. Stans, who rejoins billets 20.10.16	Y. B.
"	21.10.16		In billets. Squadron exercised. Saddling & kit inspection.	Y. B.
"	22.10.16		In billets.	Y. B.
"	23.10.16		In billets. Squadron training. Subalterns class under 2nd in command. Improvements to billets & stables.	Y. B.
"	24.10.16		In billets. Squadron training. Instruction of Subaltern Officers, Rifle Drills. Improvements to billets & stables.	Y. B.
"	25.10.16		In billets. Squadron training. Instruction of Subaltern Officers. Riding School. Improvements to billets & stables. Working party of 8 N.C.O.s men proceed to MONTREUIL for unloading Building material & billeted in SAW MILLS MONTREUIL.	Y. B.

WAR DIARY
or
INTELLIGENCE SUMMARY.

(Erase heading not required.)

Army Form C. 2118.

Place	Date	Hour	Summary of Events and Information	Remarks and references to Appendices
MERLIMONT PLAGE	26.10.16		In billets. Squadron training. Instruction of battalion officers - Musketry. Improvements to billets & stables.	
"	27.10.16		In billets. Squadron training. Instruction of battalion officers. Improvements to billets & stables.	
"	28.10.16		In billets. Squadron training. Saddling & bit-inspection. Improvements to billets & stables.	
"	29.10.16		In billets. Regiment attended Divine Service at MERLIMONT.	
"	30.10.16		In billets. Squadron training. Instruction of battalion officers. Improvements to billets & stables.	
"	31.10.16		In billets. Squadron training. Instruction of battalion officers. Improvements to billets & stables.	

Holmes
COLONEL.
COMMANDING NORTH SOMERSET YEOMANRY.

Vol 19

WAR DIARY.

NORTH SOMERSET YEOMANRY.

1st to 30th November 1916.

VOL. 25

Army Form C. 2118.

WAR DIARY
INTELLIGENCE SUMMARY.
(Erase heading not required)

NORTH SOMERSET YEOMANRY

Place	Date	Hour	Summary of Events and Information	Remarks and references to Appendices
MERLIMONT PLAGE.	1.11.16		In billets. Squadron training - Subalterns class. Improvements to billets & stables.	In.R.
"	2.11.16		In billets. Squadron training - Subalterns class - Improvements to billets & stables.	In.R.
"	3.11.16		In billets. Squadron training - Subalterns class - Improvements to billets & stables.	In.R.
"	4.11.16		In billets. Squadron exercises - Saddlery & kit inspections.	In.R.
"	5.11.16		In billets. Regiment attended Divine Service - 2/Lt. M. O'Callaghan proceeded to join 3rd Cav: Div: Working Party attached 2nd Lifegds.	In.R.
"	6.11.16		In billets. Riding School - Rifle & Regimental exercises.	In.R.
"	7.11.16		In billets. Manœuvres on Sands. Lectures to Squadrons by Squadron Leaders. 2/Lt. W.S. Salmond rejoined from 3rd Cav: Div: Working Party attached 2' Lifegds.	In.R.
"	8.11.16		In billets. Squadron exercises. Lecture to officers by 2' in command.	In.R.

Army Form C. 2118.

WAR DIARY
INTELLIGENCE SUMMARY.
(Erase heading not required.)

NORTH SOMERSET YEOMANRY

Instructions regarding War Diaries and Intelligence Summaries are contained in F. S. Regs., Part II. and the Staff Manual respectively. Title pages will be prepared in manuscript.

Place	Date	Hour	Summary of Events and Information	Remarks and references to Appendices
MERLIMONT PLAGE	9.11.16		La Villette. Regiment practised crossing trenches near BOIS du VERTON	ynl
"	10.11.16		La Villette. Manœuvres on Sands - Lecture L Squadron by Veterinary Officer.	ynl
"	11.11.16		La Villette. Riding School - Saddling & Kit inspection. Working party attached 3rd Cav. Div. Working party reprieved from 2 troops	ynl
"	12.11.16		La Villette. Regiment attended Divine Service	ynl
"	13.11.16		La Villette. Squadrons exercised - Lectures. Physical Drill. Rifle & Bayonet exercises.	ynl
"	14.11.16		La Villette. Riding School. Lectures.	ynl
"	15.11.16		La Villette. Regimental Drill & Manœuvres on Sands. Lectures.	ynl
"	16.11.16		La Villette. Regimental Drill & Manœuvres on Sands in Marching order. Lectures.	ynl
"	17.11.16		La Villette. D. Squadron on Trench Digging near BOIS du VERTON. B & C Sqns Squadron Training.	ynl
"	18.11.16		La Villette. Riding School - Saddling & Kit inspections.	ynl

WAR DIARY
INTELLIGENCE SUMMARY
(Erase heading not required.)

NORTH SOMERSET YEOMANRY

Army Form C. 2118.

Place	Date	Hour	Summary of Events and Information	Remarks and references to Appendices
MERLIMONT PLAGE	19.11.16	In billets.	Regiment attended Divine Service.	Ind?
"	20.11.16	In billets.	Squadron training and Riding School.	Ind?
"	21.11.16	In billets.	Squadron training — Riding School. Physical drill. Rifle & Bayonet exercise.	Ind?
"	22.11.16	In billets.	Squadron training — Riding School.	Ind?
"	23.11.16	In billets.	Inspection of the Regiment in Marching order by Comdg Officer.	Ind?
"	24.11.16	In billets.	Regimental drill. Manoeuvre on sands.	Ind?
"	25.11.16	In billets.	Riding School — Saddling. Kit Inspection.	Ind?
"	26.11.16	In billets.	"	Ind?
"	27.11.16	In billets.	Squadron drill. Manoeuvres on sands. Squads Class. Rifle & Bayonet exercise.	Ind?
"	28.11.16	In billets.	"	Ind?
"	29.11.16	In billets.	'B' Squadron Manoeuvre on sands. H & C Squadrons Riding School.	Ind?
"	30.11.16	In billets.	" " " " " Sig. Class. Rifle.	Ind?

M. Backhouse
Lt. Colonel.
Comdg North Somerset Yeomanry.

Vol 20

WAR DIARY.

NORTH SOMERSET YEOMANRY
1st – 31st DECEMBER 1916

VOL 20

NORTH SOMERSET YEOMANRY

WAR DIARY
or
INTELLIGENCE SUMMARY.
(Erase heading not required.)

Army Form C. 2118.

Instructions regarding War Diaries and Intelligence Summaries are contained in F.S. Regs., Part II. and the Staff Manual respectively. Title pages will be prepared in manuscript.

Place.	Hour, Date, Place Date.	Summary of Events and Information	Remarks and references to Appendices
Merlimont Plage. (in billets.)	1-12-16.	T/Major J.A. Garton relinquishes temporary rank of major & transferred to B.Sqdn.	
	6-12-16.	G.O.C. inspects Regiment crossing trenches nr. BOIS DE VERTON.	
	12-12-16.	2Lt. C.S. Campbell evacuated to hospital.	
	14-12-16.	G.O.C. inspects Regiment in full marching order on sands at MERLIMONT PLAGE.	
	15-12-16.	Capt.R. Marshall. R.A.M.C. (Attached.) evacuated to hospital.	
	16-12-16.	Billets inspected by Major-General Vaughan C.B. D.S.O.	
	20-12-16.	6th Cav. Pioneer Batt. entrained. Lt-Col. M.R.C.Backhose D.S.O. in command. Lt.Pinn, Adjutant. N.S.Y. Company Officers, Capt. J.A. Garton M.C. in command. 2nd Lieut. R.J.N. Taylor, 2nd Lt. R.E.F. Courage, 2nd Lt. K.G. Jenkins, 2nd Lt. M.A. O'Callaghan, 2nd Lt. O.M. Dodington, 2nd Lt. B. Bellott. & 261 other ranks.	
OFFIN. (in billets.)	22-12-16.	Regiment moved to new area. H.Q. & A. Sqdn. to OFFIN, B.Sqdn. to BEAURAIN CHATEAU. C. Sqdn to LOISON.	
	25-12-16.	Capt. W.A. Kennard D.S.O. 13th Hussars, promoted Major.	

COMMANDING NORTH SOMERSET YEOMANRY.

Army Form C. 2118.

Vol 21

WAR DIARY
NORTH SOMERSET YEOMANRY.
INTELLIGENCE SUMMARY.
(Erase heading not required.)

Instructions regarding War Diaries and Intelligence Summaries are contained in F.S. Regs., Part II. and the Staff Manual respectively. Title pages will be prepared in manuscript.

Hour, Date, Place	Summary of Events and Information	Remarks and references to Appendices
OFFIN. (Pas de CALAIS.) 1-1-1917.	6th Cavalry Pioneer Battalion attached for duty to 13th Corps. IN COMMAND :- Lieut-Col. M.R.C. BACKHOUSE, D.S.O. ADJUTANT, Lieut. T.A. PINN. IN COMMAND of N.S.Y. Company, 2nd Lieut. K.G. JENKINS. MAJOR C.H. DELMEGE in command of NORTH SOMERSET YEOMANRY. Captain J.A. GARTON M.C. who was in command of N.S.Y. Company admitted to hospital.	
2-1-1917.	Lieut. H.W. POPE M.C. 7th DRAGOON GUARDS joined from INDIAN CAVALRY.	
4-1-1917.	Lieut-Col. G.C. GLYN. C.M.G. D.S.O. T.D. Lieut-Col. M.R.C. BACKHOUSE D.S.O. and No. 676 S.Q.M.S. PANKHURST C.J. MENTIONED IN DESPATCHES. LONDON GAZETTE dated 4-1-17.	CJ.
5-1-1917.	2nd Lieut. C.S. CAMPBELL evacuated sick to ENGLAND struck off the strength. 2nd Lieut. W.G. SALMOND relinquishes his commission on appointment to the NEW ZEALAND FORCES.	
13-1-1917.	Maréchal des Logis PIERRE D'HEURSEL struck off the strength.	
14-1-1917.	2nd Lieut. B. BELLOT rejoined from the 6th Cavalry Pioneer Battalion.	
17-1-1917.	Captain J.A. GARTON, M.C. struck off the strength.	
22-1-1917.	Lieut. A.J.M. RICHARDSON relieved 2nd Lieut. K.G. JENKINS and took over command of N.S.Y. Company, 6th Cavalry Pioneer Battalion.	
8-2-1917.		

[signature]
MAJOR,
Commanding, NORTH SOMERSET YEOMANRY.

Army Form C. 2118.

WAR DIARY or INTELLIGENCE SUMMARY.

NORTH SOMERSET YEOMANRY.

(Erase heading not required.)

Instructions regarding War Diaries and Intelligence Summaries are contained in F.S. Regs, Part II. and the Staff Manual respectively. Title pages will be prepared in manuscript.

Hour, Date, Place	Summary of Events and Information	Remarks and references to Appendices
O.T.IN. (P-s de CALAIS.) 22-1-1917.	The following announcement appeared in the LONDON GAZETTE dated 22-1-17. No. 91 S.S.M. GOODMAN F. No. 290 Sgt. BRITTEN H. No. 1368 Sgt. HARDING S.L. No. 890 Pte BUXTON E.J. No. 1276 Pte HAM W.L. Awarded Military Medal for Bravery in the Field.	
25-1-1917.	Captain R. MARSHALL, R.A.M.C. evacuated to ENGLAND sick, struck off the strength. (17-1-17.)	
30-1-1917.	MAJOR C.H. DELMEGE took over command of the 6th Cavalry Pioneer Battalion from Lieut-Col. M.R.C. BACKHOUSE. D.S.O.	
8-2-1917.	[signature] R West MAJOR, Commanding, NORTH SOMERSET YEOMANRY.	

Vol 22

WAR DIARY

NORTH SOMERSET YEOMANRY.

1ST to 28TH FEBRUARY 1917.

VOL. No 28.

WAR DIARY or INTELLIGENCE SUMMARY

Army Form C. 2118

Instructions regarding War Diaries and Intelligence Summaries are contained in F.S. Regs., Part II. and the Staff Manual respectively. Title Pages will be prepared in manuscript. NORTH SOMERSET YEOMANRY.

(Erase heading not required.)

Place	Date	Hour	Summary of Events and Information	Remarks and references to Appendices
OFFIN.	1/2/17.		2/Lieuts. B. BULLOT, and K.G. JENKINS, V.C. RICE, and W.H.L. SHEPPARD commenced course of Instruction at the 3rd Divisional School.	ynl
"	8/2/17.		2/Lieut. R.J.M. TAYLOR rejoined from 6th Cavalry Pioneer Battn.	ynl
"	11/2/17.		2/Lieut. R.J.M. TAYLOR admitted to hospital.	ynl
"	12/2/17.		2/Lieut. F.M.L. WHISH proceeded to 6th Cavalry Pioneer Battalion. 2/Lieut. R.E.F. COURAGE rejoined from 6th Cavalry Pioneer Battn.	ynl
"	13/2/17.		2/Lieut. R.J.M. TAYLOR transferred to ENGLAND - SICK.	ynl
"	14/2/17.		MAJOR R.A. WEST and 2/Lieut. C.J. HANNAN commenced course at ANTI-GAS SCHOOL. MAJOR C.M. DELLAGE (21st LANCERS) attd. N.S.Y. and Lieut. & Adjutant, T.A. PINE, rejoined from 6th Cavalry Pioneer Battn.	ynl
"	15/2/17.		NO. 245 S.S.M. WATTS T.P. proceeded to CAMIERS to attend Musketry Course at M.G. School. 2/Lieut. W.B. STARKY and R.E.F. COURAGE temporarily attached 3rd Infty Divsn. for tour in front line trenches.	ynl
"	17/2/17.		MAJOR R.A. WEST and 2/Lieut. C.J. HANNAN rejoined from ANTI-GAS SCHOOL. The A.D. Signals, Cavalry Corps, inspected the Signallers of the Regiment, near BEAURAINVILLE.	ynl
"	18/2/17.		NO. 484 SGT. REED F. commenced course at Anti-Gas School.	ynl
"	22/2/17.		NO. 1003 PTE. POWELL M.F. died of Pneumonia at The 2nd/1-st NORTHUMBRIAN CASUALTY CLEARING STATION. DOULLENS.	ynl
"	23/2/17.		The O.C., 3rd Signal Squadron inspected the Signallers of the Regiment at OFFIN. NO. 484 SGT. F. REED rejoined from Anti-Gas School.	ynl
"	24/2/17.		G.O.C., 3rd Cavalry Division inspected the horses of C. SQUADRON at LOISON.	ynl

27/2/17.............

1875 Wt. W593/826 1,000,000 4/15 J.B.C. & A. A.D.S.S./Forms/C. 2118.

WAR DIARY
INTELLIGENCE/SUMMARY

NORTH SOMERSET YEOMANRY.

Army Form C. 2118.

Instructions regarding War Diaries and Intelligence Summaries are contained in F. S. Regs., Part II. and the Staff Manual respectively. Title pages will be prepared in manuscript.

(Erase heading not required.)

Place	Date	Hour	Summary of Events and Information	Remarks and references to Appendices
OFFIN	27/2/17.		The G.O.C. 6th Cavalry Brigade inspected the horses of A.Squadron at OFFIN. 2/Lieuts. W.D. STARKY and R.E.F. COURAGE rejoined from attachment to the 3rd Infantry DIVISION.	

Holmes
MAJOR,
Commanding, North Somerset Yeomanry.

YM 23

War Diary.
North Somerset Yeomanry.
1st to 31st March, 1917.
Volume No. 29.

WAR DIARY
INTELLIGENCE SUMMARY

(Erase heading not required.)

Army Form C. 2118.

North Somerset Yeomanry

Instructions regarding War Diaries and Intelligence Summaries are contained in F.S. Regs., Part II. and the Staff Manual respectively. Title pages will be prepared in manuscript.

Place	Hour, Date	Summary of Events and Information	Remarks and references to Appendices
OFFIN	1-3-1917	Brigadier & Adjutant (French Army) struck off the strength.	
	4-3-1917	2/Lieuts. B.M. Shifford & K.G. Jenkins, B. Kellett & 15 O.Rees, & 1 other Rank & Horses rejoined from 3rd Cavalry Division School.	
	6-3-1917	G.O.C. 6th Cavalry Brigade inspected A Squadron horses at OFFIN. Marshal de Foye Basil Friche (interpreter) French Army killed result of an accident.	Glo.
	7-3-1917	Lieut. H.V. Tippets late 9th Dragoon Guards, 2/Lt. G. Babington, 2/Lt. R. S. Burroughs & 1 O.R. & 1 Duttings proceeded to 3rd Cavalry School. 2/Lt. Seaward (French Army) taken on strength. Made Foye. Seaward A.D.C. proceeded to England. Lt. Colonel Wyld to Buckburner	
	9-3-1917	General of the late Marshal de Foye Basil Friche buried at 10.30 A.M. after Church Service.	
	11-3-17	Pioneer horses at 3rd & 5th Squadrons etc. 2/Lieut. K. G. Jenkins and 12 O.R. proceeded. Lieut Q.M. W. Wickham proceeded to 6 Cavalry Res. Battn.	

Army Form C. 2118.

WAR DIARY NORTH SOMERSET YEOMANRY.

INTELLIGENCE SUMMARY.

(Erase heading not required.)

Instructions regarding War Diaries and Intelligence Summaries are contained in F.S. Regs., Part II. and the Staff Manual respectively. Title pages will be prepared in manuscript.

Hour, Date, Place	Summary of Events and Information	Remarks and references to Appendices
OFFIN 13. 3. 1917	2nd Lieut S W LINDREA and Lieut O L REES WILLIAMS joined the Regiment from the Base with 14 other Ranks.	
16. 3. 1917	2nd Lieut M. L. Biggs rejoined from Cavalry Corps Signals School course of Signalling. Lieut Qr.Mr. W. Shakespeare, 2nd Lieut J.H. Shoel, 2nd Lieut M.A. O'Callaghan, 2nd Lieut O M Carrington, Lieut R. J. Richardson and 235 Other Ranks rejoined from 6th Cavalry Reserve Regiment.	W.
19. 3. 1917	2/Lieut K.G. Jenkins, 12th R rejoined from France on leave. Major C. St Aubyn proceeded to England on 10 days leave.	
20. 3. 1917	Lieut J W Applegate M.o. 2nd Lieut C. I. Campbell and 8 O.R. rejoined from the Base. Major Sir A. Ing. D. I.O. Queen's Bays resumed command of the Regiment and taken on the strength. Lieut R. C. B. Yolde transferred from 16 to R Squadron.	

Geo Wh... ... 9/5/.
Major ....
COMMANDING NORTH SOMERSET YEOMANRY.

WAR DIARY NORTH SOMERSET YEOMANRY

INTELLIGENCE SUMMARY

Army Form C. 2118.

Hour, Date, Place	Summary of Events and Information	Remarks and references to Appendices
OFFIN. 21.3.1917	Lieut. A.W. Pope, M.C., 2nd Lt. Babington, 2nd Lieut S.A. Hutchings, 2nd Lt. T. Savage, rejoined from the 3rd Cavalry Divisional depot.	
22.3.1917	Brigade Route march, less Echelons A & B.	
25.3.1917	Checks put forward but dinner time. 2nd Lieut. Stlington & 40 O.R.'s whrks proceeded to 1/4th Division VII Corps as a digging party.	9/10.
26.3.1917	Lieut + Adjutant T.A. Pinn granted 10 days leave to England.	
27.3.1917	2nd Lieut A.H. Wilshish & 33 O.R. whunts proceeded to join previous digging party with VII Corps making a total of 2 Officers & 73 O.R. whranks.	

2.4.1917.

COMMANDING NORTH SOMERSET YEOMANRY.

Vol 24

WAR DIARY.

NORTH SOMERSET YEOMANRY

1ST to 30TH APRIL 1917.

VOL: Nº 30.

WAR DIARY or **INTELLIGENCE SUMMARY**

Army Form C. 2118

NORTH SOMERSET YEOMANRY.

Instructions regarding War Diaries and Intelligence Summaries are contained in F.S. Regs., Part II. and the Staff Manual respectively. Title Pages will be prepared in manuscript. **1st to 30th APRIL, 1917.**

(Erase heading not required.)

Place	Date	Hour	Summary of Events and Information	Remarks and references to Appendices
OFFIN.	1-4-17.		Major-General J. VAUGHAN. C.B., D.S.O. Commanding 3rd Cavalry Division presented the ribands of the Military Medal to the following N.C.O's and men of the Regiment at MARESQUEL. No. 245 S.S.M. WATTS T.P. No. 91 S.S.M. GOODMAN F.A. No. 1368 Pte HARDING S.L. No. 890 Pte BUXTON E.J.	
do.	4-4-17.		Major C.H. Delmege proceeded to FREVENT to take command of the Cavalry Corps Reinforcement Camp.	
do.	5-4-17.		The Regiment marched at 9.20 a.m. to AUBIN ST VAAST for concentration of 6th Cav. Bde. 2nd Lieut. F.T. TURPIN joined. Following Officers supernumery to establishment proceeded to the Base :- 2nd Lieuts. M.A. O'Callaghan. O.L. Rees Williams and F.T. Turpin.	
AUBIN ST VAAST.	7-4-17.		Regiment marched at 9.15 a.m. with 6th Cav. Bde. to FORTEL via X Roads north of the A of St AUSTREBERTHE-WAIL-CONCHY-sur-CANCHE.	
FORTEL.	8-4-17.		Regiment marched at 2.30 p.m. to FOSSEUX via cross roads ARBRE-southern outskirts of REBREUVIETTE-IVERVNY-SUS ST LEGER-SOMBRIN.	
FOSSEUX.	9-4-17.		Regiment marched eastwards at 11 a.m. and arrived in ARRAS about 4 p.m. where the Regiment remained until 11 p.m. The head of the Brigade at G.23.c.6.1. Received orders about 8.30 p.m. to bivouac in ARRAS in a Factory Yard at H.22. d.6.8. Regiment off-saddled. Orders received about 10.30 p.m. to move back to L.10.c.3.0. Marched at 11.15 p.m. and arrived 12.30 a.m. 10-4-17. Snow falling heavily. Regiment off-saddled in a field and bivouaced. Orders received to be ready to move at 1 hours' notice.	
	10-4-17.		Moved at 11 a.m., snowing heavily along the main road to ARRAS and on into H.31.a where the Brigade halted. The 8th Cav. Bde. were immediately on our north here. We remained here until 2.30 p.m. when we moved up the Cavalry Track in rear of the 8th Brigade to N.3.b. where the Brigade was extended about in troop columns. It snowed hard all the afternoon and evening. About 8 p.m. we were shelled considerably and the Regiment led back to H.32.d. where the night was spent in shell holes, horses remaining saddled-up. Horses last watered at 8 a.m. this morning.	

WAR DIARY or INTELLIGENCE SUMMARY

Army Form C. 2118

NORTH SOMERSET YEOMANRY.

Instructions regarding War Diaries and Intelligence Summaries are contained in F.S. Regs., Part II. and the Staff Manual respectively. Title Pages will be prepared in manuscript.

1st to 30th APRIL, 1917.

(Erase heading not required.)

Place	Date	Hour	Summary of Events and Information	Remarks and references to Appendices
	10-4-17.		2nd Lieut. Hutchings evacuated to hospital with German Measles.	
	11-4-17.		Stood-to at 5 a.m. Shelled considerably between six and seven a.m. and had the following casualties :- Officers wounded, Major W.A. Kennard, D.S.O. Lieut.S.W. Applegate, M.C. 2nd Lieut. K.G. Jenkins, 2nd Lieut. J.H. Hewes. 4 others ranks killed, 14 other ranks wounded, 19 horses killed and wounded. All wounded casualties were evacuated to the ARRAS-CAMBRAI Road. About 8 a.m. we moved up again to N.3.b. with the remaineder of the 6th Cav.Bde. About 10 a.m. the 3rd Dragoon Guards advanced eastward over the ridge in N.4. and N.5. and they dug-in on a line running from the southern end of MONCHY to the ARRAS-CAMBRAI Road about LA BERGERE FARM. The Germans were in the enclosures on the eastern side of MONCHY and were also holding GUEMAPPE and WANCOURT on the south and from both the latter places they had direct observation. About 10.30 a.m. the remainder of the 6th Cav. Bde (1st Royal Dragoons, North Somerset Yeomanry and 6th Machine Gun Sqdn.) moved up to just below the crest in N.4.d. where they remained until about 2.30 p.m. when they were shelld out and moved back to N.3. Just before 3 p.m. B.Squadron, North Somerset Yeomanry under Major R.A. WEST with 6th Machine Gun Sqdn moved up to support the 3rd Dragoon Guards. They advanced dismounted. Major West's report on the action of his Squadron is attached hereto as an appendix. *(marked APPENDIX A)* About 7 p.m. the 6th Brigade less the 3rd Dragoon Guards and one squadron N.S.Y. and Machine Gun Squadron was again shelled out of N.3. The North Somerset Yeomanry moved north about 400 yards. The German shelling was accurate as he had direct observation from WANCOURT Tower and GUEMAPPE, but luckily he had net the weight of guns to do much damage. The 6th Cav. Bde. Dismounted party were relieved about 1.30 A.m. 12th APRIL, they returned to their horses in N.3. in a blizzard of snow and rain, everyone wet through.,The Regiment moved down the Cavalry Track back to ARRAS Race Course in L.17. where the whole of the 3rd Cavalry Division were bivouaced, reaching there about 3.30 a.m. The horses were then watered for the first time for 40 hours. The Race Course was a mass of mud and the blizzard continued throughout the night.	
	12-4-1917.		The Regiment marched at 9.30 a.m. to FOSSEUX going into the same camp it left on the 9th instant.	

Army Form C. 2118

WAR DIARY
or
INTELLIGENCE SUMMARY

(Erase heading not required.)

NORTH SOMERSET YEOMANRY.

Instructions regarding War Diaries and Intelligence Summaries are contained in F. S. Regs., Part II. and the Staff Manual respectively. Title Pages will be prepared in manuscript.

1st to 30th APRIL, 1917.

Place	Date	Hour	Summary of Events and Information	Remarks and references to Appendices
FOSSEUX.	12-4-1917.		Lieut. A.J.M. Richardson was evacuated to hospital suffering from the exposure of the previous three days. LIST OF OFFICERS who took part in operations & his wire that attached marked APPENDIX 'B'	
	13-4-1917.		Remained in Camp at FOSSEUX. A large number of men reported sick with Trench Feet, 15 were evacuated to hospital.	
do.	14-4-1917.		The Commanding Officer (Lieut-Col. G.H.A. Ing. D.S.O.) and several Officers of the Regiment attended the funeral of Brig. General. Buckley Johnson at GOUY-en-ARTOIS. It rained most of the day.	
do.	15-4-1917.		Remained in camp at FOSSEUX. Regiment attended Divine Service.	
do.	16-4-1917.		Regiment marched at 8 a.m. with the Brigade and billeted at LA BROYE. Route:- SOMBRIN-SOUS St LEGER-INVERGNY- southern outskirts BONNIERES-VILLERS L'HOPITAL-WAVANS-AUXI-le-CHATEAU.	
LA BROYE.	17-4-1917.		Remained in billets.	
do.	18-4-1917.		The Corps Commander visited the Regiment. The Divisional Commander visited the Regiment. B. Squadron under Major. R.A. West paraded for the Divisional Commander who complimented them on the way in which they had carried out their work whilst supporting the 3rd Dragoon Guards on the 11th instant.	
do.	19-4-1917.		Regiment marched west via RAYE-sur-AUTHIE to NAMPONT ST MARTIN and billeted in very comfortable billets. The Regiment lost no horses from exposure during the intensely cold weather experienced from the 9th to the 12th instant, and had no case of a sore back from the time the Regiment left OFFIN on the 5th instant to reaching these billets.	
NAMPONT ST MARTIN.	22-4-1917.		Regiment attended Divine Service. Following message received by the Corps Commander from the G.O.C. Third Army. " The G.O.C. Third Army has informed me of the good work done by the troops of the Cavalry Corps engaged in the recent fighting. Please convey to them my congratulations and especially to those Regiments which gave such valuable help in securing	

WAR DIARY or INTELLIGENCE SUMMARY.

NORTH SOMERSET YEOMANRY.

Army Form C. 2118.

(Erase heading not required.)

1st to 30th APRIL, 1917.

Place	Date	Hour	Summary of Events and Information	Remarks and references to Appendices
	22-4-1917.		and holding MONCHY-le-PREUX." Majos W.A. Major W.A. Kennard D.S.O. rejoined from hospital. 10 other ranks joined as reinforcements. 2nd Lieut. F.H.L. Whish and 46 other ranks rejoined from 3rd Cavalry Division Digging Party, 21-4-1917. 2nd Lieut. R.E.F. Courage and 15 other ranks rejoined from Cavalry Corps Re-inforcement Camp, 21-4-1917. 2nd Lieut. E.A. Hutchings rejoined from hospital 21-4-1917.	
NAMPONT ST MARTIN.	24-4-1917.		2nd Lieut. O.M. Dodington and 19 other ranks rejoined from Cavalry Corps Re-inforcement Camp.	
do.	28-4-1917.		The G.O.C. 6th Cavalry Brigade and the O.C. A.S.C. 3rd Cavalry Division inspected the A. & B. Echelons of the Regimental Transport at ROUSSENT at 10 a.m. Captain G.M. GIBBS joined from England.	
do.	29-4-1917.		Regiment attended Divine Service. 30 Remounts joined from BOULOGNE.	
do.	30-4-1917.		The G.C.C. 6th Cav. Bde. inspected the horses of the Regiment at NAMPONT ST MARTIN at 11 a.m. 18 other ranks joined as re-inforcements.	

Army Form C. 2118

APPENDIX A

NORTH SOMERSET YEOMANRY.

Instructions regarding War Diaries and Intelligence Summaries are contained in F. S. Regs., Part II. and the Staff Manual respectively. Title Pages will be prepared in manuscript.

WAR DIARY
or
INTELLIGENCE SUMMARY
(Erase heading not required.)

1st to 30th, APRIL, 1917.

Place	Date	Hour	Summary of Events and Information	Remarks and references to Appendices
	11-4-17.		Ref. Map. 51b. 1/40,000. About 3 p.m. on the 11th April I received orders from Lt-Col. G.H.A. Ing. D.S.O. at H.33.d. to proceed with my squadron dismounted to support Lt-Col. Burt D.S.O. 3rd Dragoon Guards who was holding the line from the S of MONCHY to LA BERGERE. I immediately sent Lt. Pope. M.G. forward with orders to proceed as far as possible mounted and then go forward on foot and report to Lt-Col Burt that I was bringing up B.Squadron up to his support, also to get the situation as far as possible so that I should have it on arrival. Ten minutes later I advanced with B.Squadron on foot, the Hotchkiss Guns and tool packs on pack horses. On reaching 6th Cav.Bde H.Q. (N.S.a.) I eff loaded the packs and sent the horses back and proceeded in half troops at about 2oo yards interval to the 3rd D.G's H.Q. about 3oo yards N. of LES FOSSES FARM. Having got the situation from Lt-Col. Burt, I sent Nos. 1 & 2 troops under Lt. Pope to LA BERGERE FARM, also 1 M.G. under 2Lt EMMS. M.G.C. Leaving Nos. 3 & 4 troops and one M.G. under Lt. Richardson near the 3rd D.G's H.Q. in reserve at Lt-Col. Burt's request, I then went up to LA BERGERE. The British front line then crossed the ARRAS,CAMBRAI road about 50yards E. of the X roads at LA BERGERE running N. & S.,on the S. side running through pt. 75. and thence onwards towards WANCOURT. North of the ARRAS-CAMBRAI read the line was held by the 3rd D.G's and Infantry. South of the ARRAS-CAMBRAI road the line was held by only a few details of the 6th Bedford Regt-North Lancs. Regt. East Lancs. Regt. and Warwick Regt. in all about 25. No officers or N.C.O. were present. They were very short of ammunition, several men whom I questioned having only 5 or 10 rounds. Their right flank was entirely in the air. A Private in the 6th Bedford Regt. (name since ascertained to be) had done most excellent service, making other men use captured German rifles and ammunition, in order to save their own and had instructed them in throwing German bombs. The trench line was a captured German one, very shallow, no dug-outs, no wire and our men were naturally holding it the reverse way. I decided to go back to the 3rd D.G's H.Q. to report situation to Lt-Col. Burt and get more ammunition, leaving Lt. Pope in charge. Before I left Lt. Tisdale M.G.C. arrived with 2 M.G&s, having been delayed by casualties on the way up. On my arrival at the 3rd D.G's H.Q. I found Lt-Col. Burt had sent Lt Richardson and the two troops I had left in reserve forward to assist in the consolidation of the line held by the 3rd D.G's. The line South of the ARRAS,CAMBRAI Road to point 75 being now re-inforced by 3 M.G's and 2 Hotchkiss Rifles and 2 troops N.S.Y. I placed a post of 1 Hotchkiss	

1875 Wt. W593/826 1,000,000 4/15 J.B.C. & A. A.D.S.S./Forms/C.2118.

NORTH SOMERSET YEOMANRY.

WAR DIARY or INTELLIGENCE SUMMARY.

Army Form C. 2118.

1st to 30th APRIL, 1917.

Place	Date	Hour	Summary of Events and Information	Remarks and references to Appendices
	22-4-1917.		and holding MONCHY-le-PREUX." Mayes W.A. Major W.A. Kennard D.S.O. rejoined from hospital. 10 other ranks joined as re-inforcements. 2nd Lieut. F.H.L. Whish and 46 other ranks rejoined from 3rd Cavalry Division Digging Party, 21-4-1917. 2nd Lieut. R.E.F. Courage and 15 other ranks rejoined from Cavalry Corps Re-inforcement Camp, 21-4-1917. 2nd Lieut. E.A. Hutchings rejoined from hospital 21-4-1917.	
NAMPONT ST MARTIN.	24-4-1917.		2nd Lieut. O.M. Dedington and 19 other ranks rejoined from Cavalry Corps Re-inforcement Camp.	
do.	28-4-1917.		The G.O.C. 6th Cavalry Brigade and the O.C. A.S.C. 3rd Cavalry Division inspected the A. & B. Echelons of the Regimental Transport at ROUSSENT at 10 a.m. Captain G.M. GIBBS joined from England.	
do.	29-4-1917.		Regiment attended Divine Service. 30 Remounts joined from BOULOGNE.	
do.	30-4-1917.		The G.O.C. 6th Cav. Bde. inspected the horses of the Regiment at NAMPONT ST MARTIN at 11 a.m. 18 other ranks joined as re-inforcements.	

Army Form C. 2118

WAR DIARY
or
INTELLIGENCE SUMMARY
(Erase heading not required.)

NORTH SOMERSET YEOMANRY.

Instructions regarding War Diaries and Intelligence Summaries are contained in F.S. Regs., Part II. and the Staff Manual respectively. Title Pages will be prepared in manuscript.

1st to 30th APRIL, 1917.

APPENDIX "A"

Place	Date	Hour	Summary of Events and Information	Remarks and references to Appendices
	11-4-17.		Ref. Map. 51b. 1/40,000. About 3 p.m. on the 11th April I received orders from Lt-Col. G.H.A. Ing. D.S.O. 3rd Dragoon Guards who was holding the line from the S of MONCHY to LA BERGERE. I immediately sent Lt. Pope. M.G. forward with orders to proceed as far as possible mounted and then go forward on foot and report to Lt-Col Burt that I was bringing up B.Squadron up to his support, also to get the situation as far as possible so that I should have it on arrival. Ten minutes later I advanced with B.Squadron on foot, the Hotchkiss Guns and tool packs on pack horses. On reaching 6th Cav.Bde H.Q. (N.B.a.) I off loaded the packs and sent the horses back and proceeded in half troops at about 200 yards interval to the 3rd D.G's H.Q. about 300 yards N. of LES FOSSES FARM. Having got the situation from Lt-Col. Burt, I sent Nos. 1 & 2 troops under Lt. Pepe to LA BERGERE FARM, also 1 M.G. under 2Lt ELMS. M.G.C. Leaving Nos. 3 & 4 troops and one M.G. under Lt. Richardson near the 3rd D.G's. H.Q. in reserve at Lt-Col. Burt's request. I then went up to LA BERGERE. The British front line then crossed the ARRAS-CAMBRAI road about 50yards E. of the X roads at LA BERGERE running N. & S., on the S. side running through pt. 75, and thence onwards towards WANCOURT. North of the ARRAS-CAMBRAI road the line was held by the 3rd D.G's and Infantry. South of the ARRAS-CAMBRAI road the line was held by only a few details of the 6th Bedford Regt. North Lancs. Regt. East Lancs. Regt. and Warwick Regt. in all about 25. No officers or N.C.O. were present. They were very short of ammunition, several men whom I questioned having only 5 or 10 rounds. Their right flank was entirely in the air. A Private in the 6th Bedford Regt. (name since ascertained to be _____) had done most excellent service, making other men use captured German rifles and ammunition, in order to save their own and had instructed them in throwing German bombs. The trench line was a captured German one, very shallow, no dug-outs, no wire and our men were naturally holding it the reverse way. I decided to go back to the 3rd D.G's H.Q. to report situation to Lt-Col. Burt and get more ammunition, leaving Lt. Pepe in charge. Before I left Lt. Tisdale M.G.C. arrived with 2 M.Gës, having been delayed by casualties on the way up. On my arrival at the 3rd D.G's H.Q. I found LT-Col. Burt had sent Lt Richardson and the two troops I had left in reserve forward to assist in the consolidation of the line held by the 3rd D.G's. The line South of the ARRAS-CAMBRAI Road to point 75 being now re-inforced by 3 M.G's and 2 Hotchkiss Rifles and 2 troops N.S.Y. I placed a post of 1 Hotchkiss	

1875 Wt. W593/826 1,000,000 4/15 J.B.C. & A. A.D.S.S./Forms/C. 2118.

Army Form C. 2118

APPENDIX 'A'

WAR DIARY
or
INTELLIGENCE SUMMARY
(Erase heading not required.)

NORTH SOMERSET YEOMANRY.

Instructions regarding War Diaries and Intelligence Summaries are contained in F.S. Regs. Part II. and the Staff Manual respectively. Title Pages will be prepared in manuscript. 1st to 30th APRIL, 1917.

Place	Date	Hour	Summary of Events and Information	Remarks and references to Appendices
	11-4-1917.		Rifle and 6 men at Point 68 just S.W. of LA of LA BERGERE with orders to shoot only on the right of the line of telegraph poles running down the LA BERGERE-WANCOURT road to protect the rear of our line. As soon as the ammunition arrived under 2Lt. Hannan, I guided the party up to LA BERGERE and issued ammunition to the troops. It was now getting dusk and the German working Parties came out from GUEMAPPE and commenced work on the northern side of the village. These parties were dispersed by our M.G. and rifle fire, parties of the enemy were continually seen moving on the outskirts of WANCOURT and GUEMAPPE but were dealt with by our M.G's, while the work of consolidation progressed. We held our position from 3.30 p.m. to 1.30 a.m. on the night of the 11th/12th when we were relieved by 2 companies of the Middlesex Regt. During the whole of this period the enemy was very active and on several occasions was seen to be massing for counter-attacks, but his attacks were never allowed to develope, being instantly dealt with by our M.G. and rifle fire. All ranks showed great determination and cheerfulness under very trying circumstances as this was their third consecutive night in the open in the most severe weather.	

Sgt R A W&S Major
Comdg 'B' Sqn North Somerset Yeo.

An Mitchell Major

Comdg North Somerset Yeo.

Army Form C. 2118

WAR DIARY
or
INTELLIGENCE SUMMARY

NORTH SOMERSET YEOMANRY.

(Erase heading not required.)

APPENDIX "B"

1st to 30th. APRIL.1917.

Instructions regarding War Diaries and Intelligence Summaries are contained in F. S. Regs., Part II. and the Staff Manual respectively. Title Pages will be prepared in manuscript.

Place	Date	Hour	Summary of Events and Information	Remarks and references to Appendices
			List of officers. North Somerset Yeomanry who took part in the operations 9th to 12th APRIL,1917.	
			Lieut-Col. G.H.A.Ing. D.S.O. (2nd D.G's.) Commanding. Lieut. T.A. Pinn. (18th Hussars.) Adjutant. 2nd Lieut. G. Babington. Intelligence Officer. 2nd Lieut. M.C. Biggs. Signalling Officer. Lieut. & Q.M. W. Shakespeare. Echelon. 'A'.	
			"A" Squadron. Major. A.B. Mitchell. Capt. A.W. Phipps. Lieut. R.C.B. Gibbs. 2nd Lts. C.J. Hannan. W.H.L. Sheppard. S.W. Lindree.	
			"B" Squadron. Major R.A. West. Lieut. H.W. Dee Pepe M.C. Lt. A.J.M. Richardson. 2nd Lts. W.B. Sterky. F. Luff. K.G. Jenkins. E.A. Hutchings.	
			"C" Squadron. Major W.A. Kennard. D.S.O. (13th Hussars.) Lieut. S.W. Applegate. M.C. 2nd Lts. J.H. Howes. V.G. Rice. B. Bellet. C.S. Campbell.	

Army Form C. 2118

WAR DIARY
INTELLIGENCE SUMMARY
(Erase heading not required.)

NORTH SOMERSET YEOMANRY. Vol 25

1st to 31st MAY 1917.

Place	Date	Hour	Summary of Events and Information	Remarks and references to Appendices
NAMPONT S⊤ MARTIN.	1.5.17		IN BILLETS. Lt. Col. G.H.A. RING. D.S.O. and Capt. A.W. PHIPPS took part in a Divisional Enter- Communication Scheme as Umpires.	Yes.
"	2.5.17		Following N.C.O.s awarded decorations as immediate rewards for fighting near ARRAS on 11.4.17.:— No. 165167 Sgt L. J. PACEY. Distinguished Conduct Medal. No. 165032 A/S.S.M. A. TUCKER } Military Medal. No. 165640 A/66⁰ H.S. SYMES. }	Yes.
"	3.5.17		Major W.P. KENNARD D.S.O. 13th Hussars, rel⁰ N.S.Y. proceeded to Cavalry Corps Bridging Park for attachment.	Yes.
"	4.5.17		Lt General Sir C.T.M°M. KAVANAGH. K.C.B. C.V.O. D.S.O. Comd⁰ Cavalry Corps Presented Medal Ribbons to following N.C.O⁰s at a Brigade Parade near Pt PREAUX. No. 165167 Sgt L.J. PACEY. D.C.M. 165032 A/S.S.M. A. TUCKER } Military Medal. 165640 A/66⁰ H.S. SYMES. }	Yes.
"	6.5.17		Regiment attended Divine Service. Lt. A. J. M. RICHARDSON, 2/Lt W.H. ALLEN, N. RICHARDS, O.L. REES-WILLIAMS, F.T. TURPIN and 38 N.C.O⁰s + men proceeded from the Base as reinforcements.	Yes.

1875 W₁ W593/826 1,000,000 4/15 J.B.C.&A. A.D.S.S./Forms/C. 2118.

WAR DIARY
INTELLIGENCE SUMMARY

Army Form C. 2118

Place	Date	Hour	Summary of Events and Information	Remarks and references to Appendices
NAMPONT ST MARTIN	8.5.17		IN BILLETS. The D.D.R. inspected horses of Regiment prepared for Casting. No. 165007 S.Q.M.S. S. SMITH died at ROUEN 28.4.17 from measles & trench pneumonia.	Ypd
"	10.5.17		2/Lt C.J. HANNAN to Hospital injuries received tho' his horse falling at a jump. 2/Lt M.R. O'CALLAGHAN and C. PATES joined from Base. L/t E.A. GREEN rejoined Reg.t. on ceasing to hold appointment as Intelligence Officer 6th Cavalry Bde.	Ypd
"	11.5.17		Orders received that 6th Cavalry Bde will march tomorrow 12.5.17. No. 165618 Pte BELLAMY. H. drowned whilst bathing in the River AUTHIE about 7 p.m.	Ypd
"	12.5.17		Regiment marched independently of Brigade at 9.30 a.m. to DOURIEZ via S.t PREAUX and Gillebet. Arrived DOURIEZ about 11.30 a.m. Dismounted Party, with following officers:- 2/Lt M.R. O'CALLAGHAN, O.M. DODINGTON, W.H. ALLEN, O.L. REES. WILLIAMS, & F.T. TURPIN left NAMPONT ST MARTIN by motor lorries at 1 p.m. & proceeded to BEAURAINVILLE.	Ypd
DOURIEZ	13.5.17		Regiment marched independently of Brigade at 8.30 a.m. to VILLERS L'HOPITAL via LA BROYE — GENNE IVERGNY — RUN & CHATEAU — NAVANS and Gillebet.	Ypd

Army Form C. 2118

WAR DIARY
or
INTELLIGENCE SUMMARY
(Erase heading not required.)

Instructions regarding War Diaries and Intelligence Summaries are contained in F.S. Regs., Part II. and the Staff Manual respectively. Title Pages will be prepared in manuscript.

Place	Date	Hour	Summary of Events and Information	Remarks and references to Appendices
VILLERS L'HOPITAL	14.5.17		Regiment paraded at 8.15 am and marched with Brigade to HALLOY-lès-PERNOIS via Route X Roads LE MEILLARD CHURCH — Road Junction E of BERNAVILLE — L of BERNAVILLE — CANAPLES S.E.	y.O.P.
HALLOY-lès-PERNOIS	15.5.17		Regiment paraded at 8.15 am, marched with Brigade to LA NEUVILLE & Bivouacked. Route VILLERS BOCAGE — QUERRIEU.	y.O.P.
LA NEUVILLE	16.5.17		In Bivouac. Capt. W. S. BATTEN. POOLL rejoined Reg. from Intelligence Dept.	y.O.P.
"	17.5.17		Regiment paraded at 8.30 am and marched with Bde to BAYONVILLERS via LAMOTTE-en-SANTERRE and billeted.	y.O.P.
BAYONVILLERS	18.5.17		Regiment halted. Bayonet fighting practised.	y.O.P.
"	19.5.17		Regiment paraded at 7 am and marched with Brigade to BUIRE (4 miles E of PERONNE) and Bivouacked. Route FOUCAUCOURT — VILLERS CARBONEL — BRIE — LE MESNIL BRUNTEL — CATELET — CARTIGNY STN.	y.O.P.

WAR DIARY
INTELLIGENCE SUMMARY
(Erase heading not required.)

Army Form C. 2118

Instructions regarding War Diaries and Intelligence Summaries are contained in F. S. Regs., Part II. and the Staff Manual respectively. Title Pages will be prepared in manuscript.

Place	Date	Hour	Summary of Events and Information	Remarks and references to Appendices
BUIRE	20.5.17		In bivouac.	Ynl
"	21.5.17		In bivouac. Training of Snipers, Bombers, Lewis and Bayonet fighting practice. Equitation young officers.	Ynl
"	22.5.17		Training as 21.5.17. 2/Lt C.J. Hannan rejoined from Hospital.	Ynl
"	23.5.17		Training as 21.5.17. MAJOR W.A. KENNARD D.S.O. 13th Hussars, struck off strength of NORTH SOMERSET YEOMANRY.	Ynl
"	24.5.17		MAJOR R.A. WEST & 12 Officers & 329 other ranks proceeded for duty in the trenches. A strength of this Party is attached and marked "APPENDIX A".	Ynl
"	27.5.17		2/Lts G. BABINGTON, C.J. HANNAN, B. BELLOT & W.B. STARKEY L.G. retiring LIEUTENANTS, a/1-10-16. London Gazette 23.5.17. 8 N.C.Os. and Men joined as reinforcements.	Ynl

1875 Wt. W593/826 1,000,000 4/15 J.B.C. & A. A.D.S.S./Forms/C. 2118

WAR DIARY

INTELLIGENCE SUMMARY

Army Form C. 2118

(Erase heading not required.)

Instructions regarding War Diaries and Intelligence Summaries are contained in F.S. Regs., Part II. and the Staff Manual respectively. Title Pages will be prepared in manuscript.

Place	Date	Hour	Summary of Events and Information	Remarks and references to Appendices
BUIRE.	28.5.17.		In bivouac. Lt. Col. G.C.GLYN, C.M.G., D.S.O. T.D. + Lieut. & Adjt. T.A. PINN (18th Hussars) mentioned in Sir D. Haig's Despatch. L.G. 15-5-17.	Ygd
"	30.5.17.		In bivouac. Major C.H. IDELMEGE, 21st Lancers att'd 2 N. Somerset Yeo. rejoined from Cavalry Corps Camp, FREVENT.	Ygd
"	31.5.17		In bivouac. No. 165-070. Sgt. STYLES. W.C. awarded the MEDAILLE MILITAIRE for gallantry in action on April 11th 1917 near ARRAS.	Ygd

W Wiggin Lt. Col.
Comdg. N. Somerset Yeomanry.

Army Form C. 2118

WAR DIARY
or
INTELLIGENCE SUMMARY

(Erase heading not required.)   APPENDIX A.

NORTH SOMERSET YEOMANRY.

Instructions regarding War Diaries and Intelligence Summaries are contained in F.S. Regs., Part II. and the Staff Manual respectively. Title Pages will be prepared in manuscript.

24th to 31st MAY. 1917.

Place	Date	Hour	Summary of Events and Information	Remarks and references to Appendices
BUIRE.	24-5-17.		Ref: 1/20,000 Sheets 57.c. S.E. & 62.c. N.E. Major R.A. West and 12 officers and 329 other ranks left bivouac on the evening 24th May and proceeded to EPEHY to join 6th Cav. Bde party holding D.1. Sub-sector of trench line and took over the BROWN Line from 3rd Dragoon Guards at 10.30 p.m. The following officers accompanied the party, Major A.B. Mitchell, Captain A.W. Phipps, Lieut. H.W.Pope. M.C. Lieut. E.A. Green, Lieut. W.B. Starky, 2nd Lieut. R.F. Courage, E.A. Hutchings, O.L. Rees Williams, C. Pates. Capt. H. Dunkerley. (R.A.M.C.) 2nd Lieut. V.C. Rice proceeded as Sniping Officer to the Brigade and 2nd Lieut. W.H.L. Sheppard as assistant to Capt. J. Blakiston-Houston. D.S.O. Staff Captain, 6th Cavalry Brigade. Enemy shelled EPEHY with 8 15 centimetre shells in F.l.c. There were no casualties.	
EPEHY.	25-5-1917.		Working parties were furnished from 9 a.m. to 12 noon and 3 p.m. to 5 p.m. by A. Squadron in F.2.c.9.9. improving and draining present trench system. B. & C. Squadrons repairing roads, entrances to dug-outs etc., in EPEHY. 5 Officers, 225 others ranks B. & C. Squadrons paraded at F.3.b.9.8. at 9.30 p.m. for work in GREEN Line and carried out the following work. Communication trenches to H. and G. Posts in GREEN Line. Trenches deepened and trench boards laid. The party worked from 10.45 p.m. until 2.25 a.m.	
do.	26-5-17.		Working parties employed on communication trenches to H. and G. Posts - deepening trenches and laying trench boards. Party left EPEHY at 8.30 p.m. and returned at 3.35 a.m. 27th May.	
do.	27-5-17.		Major A.B. Mitchell with 2nd Lieuts. Starky, Courage and Pates and 149 other ranks took over the BIRDCAGE, X.29.d. and X.30.c. The remaining 14 squadron under Major R.A.West took over the support to the GREEN Line. Dug-outs were constructed by this party along sunken road east of Copse 13. where two troops of B. Squadron were posted. Party of 100 men furnished by Regiment from support to GREEN Line to take trench boards to H. communication trench. 2Lieut. Hutchings and 23 men employed wiring communication trench leading from Pigeon Quarry to BIRDCAGE. Only one strand of wire laid owing to VERY Lights being sent up every few minutes and heavy shrapnel fire.	

Army Form C. 2118

WAR DIARY or INTELLIGENCE SUMMARY

NORTH SOMERSET YEOMANRY.

(Erase heading not required.) Appendix.A.

24th to 31st May.1917.

Place	Date	Hour	Summary of Events and Information	Remarks and references to Appendices
ENEMY.	27-5-17.		A/Cpl. Sign. Dunn reported missing whilst proceeding from the BIRDCAGE to GREEN Line. (Believed to be taken prisoner.)	nil
	28-5-17.		In the BIRDCAGE the early morning was quiet. At about 2.15 a.m. a party of Germans estimated at 12 showed themselves at the communication trench at a point about midway between quarries and BIRDCAGE. Our Hotchkiss Rifles opened fire and the enemy disappeared in the long grass. The Quarries were shelled at 6.30 p.m. with trench mortars and the Regiment had the following casualties :- No. 165432 Cpl. Barnett A.H. No. 165541 L/Cpl. Webber J. No. 165648 L/Cpl. Watts R.A. No. 165763 Pte Sheppard W.E. No. 165376 Pte Kettlety F. } Wounded. No. 165847 Pte Smale F. No. 165570 Pte Harris A.V. No. 165264 Pte Selman R. No. 165808 Pte Emery H. Cpl. Barnett and L/Cpl. Webber remained at Duty. During the day men not on sentry worked on improving trenches in BIRDCAGE and dug-outs in and around the Quarries. During the night 28th/29th 20 men were employed wiring on North side of communication trench to the BIRDCAGE for 4½ hours. and 40 men on the south side. 50 men worked for 4 hours improving the communication trench. There was some shrapnel fire over the Quarries and BIRDCAGE about 11.30 p.m.	nil
	29-5-1917.		BIRDCAGE, Quarries and area between shelled with shrapnel 1.45 a.m. to 2.30 a.m. probably due to digging parties having been seen. Enemy sent up a large number of flares from trenches E. and N. of BIRDCAGE.trench. The remainder of the day was quiet. 30 men of the Regiment employed during night 29/30th wiring North side of communication trench. Various fatigue parties and working parties furnished for work in the GREEN Line. About 9.5 p.m. enemy patrol of 20 men were seen to come out of German trench near where it crosses sunken road at F.6. a.4.9. and creep towards our posts at F.5.b.2.9. Machine gun fire was opened on them and they disappeared.	nil
	30-5-17.		Early morning was quiet in the BIRDCAGE. About 4.30 a.m. enemy put 30 to 35 trench mortar shells into the Quarries. Remainder of the day was quiet with the exception of some machine gun fire over the top of the Quarries from the direction of OSSUS WOOD. Working party of 100 men employed during the night 30/31st wiring on North and South sides of communication trench. 1½ squadrons in BIRDCAGE and Quarries relieved during the night by 1½ sqdns. 3rd Dragoon Guards.	nil

Army Form C. 2118.

NORTH SOMERSET YEOMANRY.

WAR DIARY or INTELLIGENCE SUMMARY.

APPENDIX.A.

(Erase heading not required.)

Instructions regarding War Diaries and Intelligence Summaries are contained in F. S. Regs., Part II. and the Staff Manual respectively. Title pages will be prepared in manuscript.   24th to 31st MAY. 1917.

Place	Date	Hour	Summary of Events and Information	Remarks and references to Appendices

	30-5-17.		1½ squadrons from BIRDCAGE and Quarries and 1½ squadrons from Support to GREEN line took over GREEN Line from 1st Royal Dragoons. These reliefs were completed by 2.30 p.m. 31st May. 17. Working parties were found during the night 30/31st May completing trench West of Copse 12, making Battalion H.Q. dug-outs and improving Hotchkiss Posts East of Little Priel Farm. Work done during 31st May.17. Trenches deepened and levelled, parapets strengthened. S.A.A. Store built for reserve ammunition. Various working parties employed throughout the day and night 31st/1st June improving trenches. A patrol of 1 sergeant and 8 men were sent out at 10.30 p.m. night 31st-1st. The patrol worked from F.5.d.O.O. in a North-easterly direction until they reached WILLOW TREES. In doing so passed through three lots of wire. They remained there 3/4 of an hour and saw no sign of the enemy.
			
			A patrol under 2nd Lieut. V.C. Rice went out on the evening of the 30th May with the idea of covering the relief of the BIRDCAGE from the direction of OSSUS WOOD. by lying up for patrols of the enemy leaving the wood. It was intended to get close up to the southern edge before the enemy put out his night outposts. This however was fustrated by the presence of a sniper in one of the trees at the western end of the wood who continued firing at the patrol. 2nd Lieut. Rice did some excellent shooting and shot the sniper who fell headlong out of the tree.
			
			Lt. E.A. GREEN left trenches sick on 28th May. Lt. B. BELL O7 and 2/Lt. F.T. TORPIN joined Tornel/July.
			
			                                           Lieut-Colonel,
			                              Commanding North Somerset Yeomanry.
				✳ X 28cmE: = F.5.d.1.1.

Vol 26

WAR DIARY

NORTH SOMERSET YEOMANRY

1st to 30th JUNE 1917

VOL. No 32.

Army Form C. 2118

WAR DIARY
or
INTELLIGENCE SUMMARY

NORTH SOMERSET YEOMANRY.

Instructions regarding War Diaries and Intelligence Summaries are contained in F. S. Regs., Part II. and the Staff Manual respectively. Title Pages will be prepared in manuscript.

1st to 30th JUNE, 1917.

(Erase heading not required.)

Place	Date	Hour	Summary of Events and Information	Remarks and references to Appendices
BUIRE.	1st June.		In bivouac. Trench party under Major R.A. WEST remained in trenches D.1. Sub-sector EAST of EPEHY.	
do.	3rd June.		In bivouac. Major R.A. WEST and trench party returned to camp at 5 a.m.	
do.	4th June.		In bivouac. Subaltern officers instructed by 2nd in Command.	
do.	5th June.		in bivouac. Training of bombers, snipers and signallers carried out. Brigade order to "Stand to" to move at 4 hours notice.	
do.	6th June.		In bivouac. Squadron training, training of bombers snipers and signallers carried out.	
do.	7th June.		In bivouac. The Regiment took part in a Brigade Scheme near VILLERS - FAUCON.	
do.	8th June.		In bivouac. Squadron training, training of bombers, snipers and signallers.	
do.	9th June.		In bivouac. Saddle and kit inspections.	
do.	10th June.		In bivouac. Regiment attended Divine Service. 12 men joined as re-inforcements from the Base. 9-6-1917.	
do.	11th June.		In bivouac. Major C. H. Delmege, 10 officers, 319 other ranks proceeded for duty in the trenches in D.2. Sub-sector EAST of EPEHY. War Diary for parties in trenches during JUNE 1917 is attached and marked Appendix A.	
do.	12th June.		Bivouac.	
do.	13th June.		In bivouac. 10 remounts joined from the Base. 2nd Lieut. F. H. L. WHISH struck off strength, invalided to England. 5-6-17.	
do.	13th June to 20th June.		In bivouac.	
do.	20th June.		In bivouac. Lieutenant-Colonel G. H. A. ING. D.S.O. and Headquarters, North Somerset Yeomanry proceeded to take over D.2. Sub-sector Headquarters east of EPEHY from H.Q. 1st Royal Dragoons.	
do.	21st June.		In bivouac. 10 remounts joined from the Base.	
do.	22nd June to 25th June		im bivouac.	
do.	26th June.		In bivouac. 2nd Lieut. V.C. Rice struck off the strength. (wounded.)	
do.	27th June to 28th June		in bivouac.	
do.	29th June.		In bivouac. Lieutenenat-Colonel G. H. A. ING. D.S.O. all officers and other ranks returned from the trenches on the 6th Cavalry Brigade being relieved by the 5th Lancers and 4th Hussars. 23 remounts joined from the Base.	
do.	30th June.		In bivouac. Saddlery and kit inspections.	

Commanding North Somerset Yeomanry.

Lieutenant-Colonel,

Army Form C. 2118

NORTH SOMERSET YEOMANRY.

Instructions regarding War Diaries and Intelligence Summaries are contained in F. S. Regs., Part II. and the Staff Manual respectively. Title Pages will be prepared in manuscript.

WAR DIARY

or

INTELLIGENCE SUMMARY

(Erase heading not required.)

Appendix. A.

1st to 30th JUNE, 1917.

Place	Date	Hour	Summary of Events and Information	Remarks and references to Appendices
Reference Map. 57c. S.E. 1/20,000.	1st June.		Trench party under Major R.A. WEST remained in INTERMEDIATE Line. Work done 1st to 2nd June, trenches deepened and levels adjusted for trench boards. Parapets strengthened with sandbags. Situation quiet. 3.30 to 5 p.m. 1st June some shrapnel burst over the trenches, no casualties.	
	2nd June.		6th Cavalry Brigade relieved in D.1. Sector by the 8th Cavalry Brigade during the night. N.S.Y. party under Major R.A. WEST returned to camp at BUIRE arriving about 5 a.m. 3rd June.	
Reference Map. Sheet 57c. S.E.	11th June.		Major C.H. DELMEGE. 10 officers and 319 other ranks proceeded for duty in the trenches with 6th Cavalry Brigade in D.2. Sub-sector East of EPEHY and relieved 3rd Dragoon Guards at 10.30 p.m. Working party of 1 officer and 28 other ranks furnished for work in L. Post INTERMEDIATE LINE under R.E. Officer.	
	12th June.		Working party of 2 officers, 95 other ranks under R.E. Officer wiring by night from 10.30 p.m. from No.1. OUTPOST to K. Post. 1 officer 64 other ranks working in communication trench from L. Post to New Outpost Headquarters.	
	13th June.		Following working parties furnished. 1 officer 65 other ranks communication trench from L.P. Post to New Outpost Headquarters.2 officers 89 other ranks wiring from No.1. Outpost to K. Post. During the afternoon, billets and bivouacs in EPEHY improved.	
	14th June.		Following working parties furnished. 1 officer 74 other ranks widening and clearing out communication trench from L. Post to New Outpost Headquarters. 2 officers 98 other ranks wiring from No.1. Outpost to K. Post.	
	15th June.		Following working parties furnished. 1 officer 74 other ranks widening and clearing out communication trench from L. Post to New Outpost Headquarters. 2 officers 98 other ranks wiring from No.1. Outpost to K. Post. Captain PHIPPS and Lieut. RICHARDSON proceeded to OUTPOST Line at 10 p.m. to look round prior to taking over on 17th/18th June.	
	16th June.		Following working parties were furnished. 1 officer 270 other ranks on communication trench X.27.b.1.9. to X.21.d.8.4. 2 officers 96 other ranks wiring K. Post to No.1. Outpost. Billets improved in EPEHY, by day.	
	17th June.		OUTPOST Line taken over from 1st Royal Dragoons night 17th/18th. 3rd Dragoon Guards relieved North Somerset Yeomanry in 2nd Line. One and a half squadrons N.S.Y. relieved one and a half	

WAR DIARY
INTELLIGENCE SUMMARY

Army Form C. 2118

NORTH SOMERSET YEOMANRY.

Instructions regarding War Diaries and Intelligence Summaries are contained in F.S. Regs, Part II. and the Staff Manual respectively. Title Pages will be prepared in manuscript.

(Erase heading not required.) Appendix A.

1st to 30th JUNE, 1917.

Place	Date	Hour	Summary of Events and Information	Remarks and references to Appendices
	17th June.		squadrons 1st Royal Dragoons in INTERMEDIATE SUPPORT LINE. A number of small shells burst in the southern quarter of the village of EPEHY during the morning. No damage done.	
	18th June.		Working party of 1 officer 60 other ranks from INTERMEDIATE SUPPORT LINE improving trenches in OUTPOST LINE. Covering party of 1 officer and 20 men furnished for wiring party in front of No.1. and No.2. OUTPOSTS.	
	19th June.		Working party furnished as one 16th June.	
	20th June.		One and a half squadrons in INTERMEDIATE SUPPORT LINE relieved the one and a half squadrons in the OUTPOST LINE.	
Lieut-Colonel.			ALWAY G.H.A. ING. D.S.O. Lieut. & Adjutant T.A.PINN and Headquarters, North Somerset Yeomanry. relieved Lieut-Col. F.W. WORMALD and Headquarters, 1st Royal Dragoons in D.2. Sub-sector Headquarters.	
	21st June.		Captain G. GIBBS, Lieut. B. Bellot, 2nd Lieuts. Starky, Sheppard and Lindree joined from Details at BUIRE. Major A.B. MITCHELL, Lieut. E.A. GREEN, 2nd Lieuts. Richards and Pates returned to Details. Working party of 3 officers, 60 other ranks from INTERMEDIATE SUPPORT LINE improving trenches in Outpost Line.	
	22nd June.		Following furnished by troops in INTERMEDIATE SUPPORT. Working party 3 officers 60 other ranks improving trenches in OUTPOST LINE. Covering party 1 officer 20 other ranks to party wiring OSSUS WOOD to CANAL WOOD.	
	23rd June.		One and a half squadrons N.S.Y. On OUTPOST LINE, one and a half squadrons N.S.Y. in INTERMEDIATE SUPPORT LINE relieved by 3rd Dragoon Guards. 3 squadrons N.S.Y. took over INTERMEDIATE LINE from 2 squadrons 1st Royal Dragoons and one squadron 3rd Dragoon Guards.	
	24th June.		Work done improving trenches in K. L. and M. Posts.	
	25th June.		Work done improving trenches K.L. and M. Posts. Working party 1 officer 40 other ranks working on communication trench L. Post to D.2. Sub-sector H.Q. PIGEON RAVINE. About 20 shells fell near K. Post between the hours of 3 p.m. and 4 p.m.	
	26th June.		Work done as on 25th instant.	
	27th June.		Work done as on June 26th. About 50 shells burst near D.2. H.Q. during the evening. No damage done.	
	28th June.		The 6th Cavalry Brigade were relieved in D.2. Sub-sector by the 5th Lancers and 4th Hussars. North Somerset Yeomanry in INTERMEDIATE SUPPORT LINE relieved by 3 squadrons 5th Lancers. Major R.A. WEST relieved Major C.H. DELMEGE night 23rd/24th June. North Somerset Yeomanry when relieved by 5th Lancers returned to Camp at BUIRE.	
			During the time the Regiment were in the trenches, 2nd Lieut. V.C. RICE and the SCOUTS of the Regiment were employed in scouting and patrolling in front of the OUTPOST LINE.	

NORTH SOMERSET YEOMANRY.

Instructions regarding War Diaries and Intelligence Summaries are contained in F.S. Regs., Part II. and the Staff Manual respectively. Title Pages will be prepared in manuscript.

WAR DIARY
INTELLIGENCE-SUMMARY.
(Erase heading not required.)

1st to 30th JUNE, 1917. Appendix A.

Army Form C. 2118

Place	Date	Hour	Summary of Events and Information	Remarks and references to Appendices
			On the night 24/25th June, a raid was carried out by the 1st Royal Dragoons. 2nd Lieut. V.C. RICE and the scouts North Somerset Yeomanry took part in this raid. "Lieut. V.C. RICE was wounded.	W

[signature] Lieutenant-Colonel,
Commanding North Somerset Yeomanry.

Vol 27

WAR DIARY.

North Somerset Yeomanry

1st to 31st July 1917.

Vol. No. 33.

Army Form C. 2118

WAR DIARY
of
INTELLIGENCE SUMMARY

(Erase heading not required.) 1st to 31st JULY 1917.

NORTH SOMERSET YEOMANRY.
Instructions regarding War Diaries and Intelligence Summaries are contained in F.S. Regs. Part II. and the Staff Manual respectively. Title Pages will be prepared in manuscript.

Place	Date	Hour	Summary of Events and Information	Remarks and references to Appendices
BUIRE	1st July.	In bivouac.	Regiment attended Divine Service, Maj.R.A.WEST proceeded to FLEXICOURT to attend a course at the Fourth Army School.	
do.	2nd July.	Inbivouac.	Dismounted party under Capt.W.S.BATTEN-POOLL attached to 2nd Cavalry Div. the following officers accompanied the party, 2nd Lieuts. O.M.DODINGTON O.L.REES WILLIAMS, and W.H.ALLEN. Total 4 Officers 63 O.R.	
do.	3rd July.	In bivouac.	Regiment paraded at 8 a.m. and marched with 6th Cav. Bde. to camp at SUZANNE. Route PERONNE - MARICOURT.	
SUZANNE	4th July	In bivouac.	Regiment paraded at 8.15 a.m. and marched with Brigade to billets and camp at HEILLY. No 155292 Sgt HOWEL E.W. awarded the MILITARY MEDAL for gallantry in action.	
HEILLY.	5th July	In bivouac.	Regiment paraded 8.45 a.m. and marched with Brigade to new billeting area. AMPLIER east of DOULLENS. Regiment bivouaced at AUTHIEULE.	
AUTHIEULE	6th July	In bivouac.	Regiment paraded at 9 a.m. and marched with Brigade to ETREE-WAMIN and bivouaced. Route LUCHEUX - IVERGNY.	
ETREE-WAMIN	7th July	In bivouac.	Regiment paraded at 9.30 a.m. and marched to new billets at LA PUGNOY.	
LA PUGNOY	8th July	In billets.		
LA PUGNOY	9th July	In billets.	The following N.C.O's. and Men wounded with Dismounted Party attached 2nd Cav.Div. near EPEHY. No.165085 L/C HOLLOWAY C.T. No.165063 Pte KELLY G. No.165847 Pte SMALES F. No.165184 Sgt HAYES F.S. (remained at duty.)	
LA PUGNOY	10th July	In billets.	Dismounted Party attached 2nd Cav.Div. rejoined the Regiment.	

Army Form C. 2118

WAR DIARY
or
INTELLIGENCE SUMMARY

(Erase heading not required.) 1st to 31st JULY 1917.

NORTH SOMERSET YEOMANRY

Instructions regarding War Diaries and Intelligence Summaries are contained in F.S. Regs., Part II. and the Staff Manual respectively. Title Pages will be prepared in manuscript.

Place	Date	Hour	Summary of Events and Information	Remarks and references to Appendices
LA PUGNOY	11th July	In billets.		
LA PUGNOY	12th July	do.	The G.O.C. 6th Cavalry Brigade inspected all Recruits and Remounts that joined the Regiment since April 11th 1917.	
LA PUGNOY	13th July	do.	Maj.R.A.WEST returned from 4th Army School FLEXICOURT.	
LA PUGNOY	14th July	do.		
LA PUGNOY	15th July	do.	Regiment attended Divine Service.	
LA PUGNOY	16th July	do.	Regiment paraded at 5 a.m. and marched to new billets in HAVERSKERQUE Area. Route CHOCQUES - ROBECQ - ST VENANT. Regimental Headquarters and B Squadron bivouaced at HAVERSKERQUE C.and A. Squadrons at LA MOTTE BAUDET. 2nd Lieut. V.C.RICE awarded MILITARY CROSS for gallantry in action	
HAVERSKERQUE	17th July	In bivouac.		
HAVERSKERQUE	18th July	do.		
HAVERSKERQUE	19th July	do.	The G.O.C. 6th Cav Bde. inspected Ai. Echelon in marching order at 10 a.m.	
HAVERSKERQUE	20th July	do.	The G.O.C. 6th Cav.Bde. inspected the Regiment less A and B Echelons in marching order at 10 a.m.	
HAVERSKERQUE	21st July	do.		
HAVERSKERQUE	22nd July	do.	Regiment attended Divine Service.	
HAVERSKERQUE	23rd July	do.	Pioneer Class under 2nd Lieut. W.H.L.SHEPPARD commenced Course under R.E. and attached to C. Battery R.H.A.	

WAR DIARY

NORTH SOMERSET YEOMANRY

Army Form C. 2118.

INTELLIGENCE SUMMARY.

(Erase heading not required.) 1st to 31st July 1917.

Instructions regarding War Diaries and Intelligence Summaries are contained in F.S. Regs., Part II. and the Staff Manual respectively. Title pages will be prepared in manuscript.

Place	Date	Hour	Summary of Events and Information	Remarks and references to Appendices
HAVERSKERQUE	24th July	In bivouac.	1 Officer, 1 N.C.O. and 2 Hotchkiss Rifle Teams per Squadron proceeded to CAMIERS for attachment to G.H.Q. S.A. School for firing and training. G.O.C. 6th Cav.Bde. inspected horses proposed for casting at 9.30 a.m.	
HAVERSKERQUE	25th July	do.		
HAVERSKERQUE	26th July	do.	Pioneer Class under 2nd Lieut.SHEPPARD rejoined Regiment owing to Course being postponed.	
HAVERSKERQUE	27th July	do.		
HAVERSKERQUE	28th July	do.	Lieut.W.B.STARKY and 3 N.C.O's. proceeded to ST POL to attend a twelve days' course at the Physical Training and Bayonet School commencing 30th July.	
HAVERSKERQUE	29th July	do.		
HAVERSKERQUE	30th July	do.	Hotchkiss Rifle Teams at CAMIERS relieved by the two remaining teams per Squadron	
HAVERSKERQUE	31st July	do.	Intelligence personnel under Maj.C.H.DELMEGE attended Brigade Intelligence Scheme.	

The following training carried out in the HAVERSKERQUE area. Equitation and Training of Remounts, Musketry, Canal Crossing, Tactical Exercises, Bayonet Fighting, Bombing, etc.

The Musketry Range at AIRE allotted to the Regiment twice a week and the 1st Army School Range at ROMBLY on the 29th inst.

Lieut.Colonel,
Commanding North Somerset Yeomanry.

Vol 28

WAR DIARY
North Somerset Yeomanry
1st to 31st August 1917.
Vol. No. 34.

Army Form C. 2118.

WAR DIARY
or
INTELLIGENCE SUMMARY.

(Erase heading not required.) 1st to 31st August 1917.

NORTH SOMERSET YEOMANRY.

Instructions regarding War Diaries and Intelligence
Summaries are contained in F.S. Regs., Part II.
and the Staff Manual respectively. Title pages
will be prepared in manuscript.

Hour, Date, Place		Summary of Events and Information	Remarks and references to Appendices
HAVERSKERQUE.	1st August.	In Billets. Training.	
do	2nd do	In Billets. Training.	
do	3rd do	In Billets. Training. "C" Squadron fired on the Range at AIRE. 2nd Lt. C. PATES & 2nd Lt. N. RICHARDS rejoined from Musketry Course at CAMIERS. 2nd Lt. R.E.F. COURAGE & Lt. C.J. HANNAN, proceeded on leave to England.	
do	4th do	In Billets. Training.	
do	5th do	In Billets. *1 Officer & 13 O.R. attending Divine Service at RANCHICOURT. 2 Officers & 50 O.R. attended Divine Service at HAVERSKERQUE.	* Special Parade Service in Commemoration of the 3rd Anniversary of the Commencement of the war [signature]
do	6th do	In Billets. Training. Divisional Rifle meeting at ROMBLY. 2nd Lt. O.L. REES WILLIAMS & 50 O.R. proceeded as dismounted working party to the 5th Army. Lieut. E.A. GREEN granted leave to England. Interpreter CHAMPAGNE h. joined for duty.	
do	7th do	In Billets. Training. 2nd Lt. C. PATES proceeded to 1st Army sniping school. 2nd Lt. E.A. HUTCHINGS rejoined from Musketry school at ROMBLY.	
do	8th do	In Billets. Training. "A" Squadron fired on the range at AIRE. Captain H. DUNKERLEY, R.A.M.C. proceeded on leave to England.	
do	9th do	In billets. Training. Lieut & Adjutant T.A. PINN, admitted to Hospital.	

WAR DIARY or **INTELLIGENCE SUMMARY**

NORTH SOMERSET YEOMANRY.

Army Form C. 2118.

(Erase heading not required.) 1st to 31st August 1917.

Place	Date	Hour	Summary of Events and Information	Remarks and references to Appendices
HAVERSKERQUE.	10th August.	In Billets.	Inspection of horses by Commanding Officer. Training. Major C.H.DELMEGE & Captain A.W.PHIPPS, proceeded on leave to England.	
do	11th do	In Billets.	2/Lieut. C. PATES rejoined from 1st Army Sniping School. Training. "B" Squadron fired on the range at AIRE.	
do	12th do	In Billets.	Regiment attended Divine Service. 2nd Lt. C.S.CAMPBELL, proceeded to 1st Army Sniping School. 2nd Lt E.A.HUTCHINGS proceeded on leave to England.	
do	13th do	In Billets.	Training. "C" Squadron fired on the range at AIRE. Lt. H.W.POPE, M.C. and 2nd Lt. M.C.BIGGS proceed on leave to England.	
do	14th do	In Billets.	Regiment carried out Canal crossing.	
do	15th do	In Billets.	Training. Instruction of Regimental Bombers under 2/Lt. F.LUFF. 2/Lt. W.H.L.Sheppard, proceeded on leave to England.	
do	16th do	In Billets.	Training. "A" Squadron fired on the range at AIRE.	
do	17th do	In Billets.	Training. 2/Lt. B.W.LINDREA proceeded on leave to England.	
do	18th do	In Billets.	Training. Lieut. W.B.STARKY rejoined from Physical Training & Bayonet School, ST POL. 2/Lt.O.M.DODINGTON, admitted to Hospital.	
do	19th do	In Billets.	Regiment attended Divine Service. Captain W.S.BATTEN-POOLL, proceeded to Labour Corps, Base Depot at BOULOGNE for duty. Struck off the strength of the Regiment. Lieut G. BABINGTON rejoined from Hospital.	
do	20th do	In Billets.	Training. Captain G.M.GIBBS & Lieut W.B.STARKY proceeded on leave to England.	
do	21st do	In Billets.	Inspection of Transport by O.C. A.S.C. Training. "B" Squadron fired on the range at AIRE.	

NORTH SOMERSET YEOMANRY.

WAR DIARY
or
INTELLIGENCE SUMMARY.
(Erase heading not required.) 1st to 31st August 1917.

Army Form C. 2118.

Hour, Date, Place			Summary of Events and Information	Remarks and references to Appendices
HAVERSKERQUE.	22nd August.	In Billets.	Training.	
do	23rd do	In Billets.	Training.	
do	24th do	In Billets.	Training. 2/Lt. W.H.ALLEN proceeded to Dismounted party 5th Army as-q for duty as quartermaster. 2/Lt. C.PATES and 2/LT. W.RICHARDS proceed on leave to England. Divisional Horse Show held at BUSNES.	
do	25th do	In Billets.	Training.	
do	26th do	In Billets.	~~Training.~~ 2/Lt. F.T.TURPIN & 50 O.R. proceeded to 5th Army in relief of 2nd Lt. O.L.REES WILLIAMS & 50 O.R. Regiment attended Divine Service. Lieut. B.BELLOT admitted to Hospital.	
do	27th do	In Billets.	Training.	
do	28th do	In Billets.	Training.	
do	29th do	In Billets.	Training. "A" Squadron fired on the range at AIRE.	
do	30th do	In Billets.	Training.	
do	31st do	In Billets.	Training. "B" Squadron fired on the range at AIRE. Major R.A.WEST proceeded on leave to England.	

Holmes Major.,
Commanding North Somerset Yeomanry.

Vol 29

WAR DIARY

North Somerset Yeomanry

1st to 30th September 1917.

Vol. No. 35

Army Form C. 2118.

WAR DIARY
or
INTELLIGENCE SUMMARY.

(Erase heading not required.)

NORTH SOMERSET YEOMANRY

1st to 30th SEPTEMBER 1917.

Place	Date	Hour	Summary of Events and Information	Remarks and references to Appendices
HAVERSKERQUE	1st September.	In Billets.	Training. 2nd Lieut C.S.CAMPBELL rejoined from 1st Army Sniping School.	
"	2nd	"	Regiment attended Divine Service.	
"	3rd	"	Training. 165292 Sgt HOWELL E.W. proceeded to 1st Army Musketry Camp at LINGHEM to attend a Course of instruction in Musketry. Lieut.& Adjutant T.A.PINN (18th Hussars) rejoined from hospital. 4 Remounts joined from the Base.	
"	4th	"	Training.	
"	5th	"	Regiment carried out a Regimental Scheme.	
"	6th	"	Training.	
"	7th	"	Training. Dispatch Riders Scheme	
"	8th	"	Training. 2nd Lieut. F.T.TURPIN wounded 6/9/17.	
"	9th	"	Regiment attended Divine Service.	
"	10th	"	Training.	
"	11th	"	Regiment carried out Regimental Scheme.	
"	12th	"	Training.	
"	13th	"	Training. Lieut.B.BELLOT rejoined from hospital. 2nd Lieut.E.A. HUTCHINGS admitted to hospital.	
"	14th	"	Training.	
"	15th	"	Training.	

Army Form C. 2118.

WAR DIARY
or
INTELLIGENCE SUMMARY.
(Erase heading not required.)

NORTH SOMERSET YEOMANRY

1st to 30th SEPTEMBER 1917.

Instructions regarding War Diaries and Intelligence Summaries are contained in F. S. Regs., Part II. and the Staff Manual respectively. Title pages will be prepared in manuscript.

Place	Date	Hour	Summary of Events and Information	Remarks and references to Appendices
HAVERSKERQUE	16th September	In Billets.	Regiment attended Divine Service.	
"	17th "	"	Regiment carried out Regimental Scheme.	
"	18th "	"	Training.	
"	19th "	"	Regiment carried out Regimental Scheme. 10 men transferred to Base.	
"	20th "	"	Training.	
"	21st "	"	Regiment took part in a Brigade Scheme. Capt.H.DUNKERLEY, R.A.M.C., proceeded for duty to the XIII Corps. No165318 Pte A.W.ROAN proceeded to England for admission to an Officers' Cadet Unit.	
"	22nd "	"	Training.	
"	23rd "	"	Regiment attended Divine Service.	
"	24th "	"	Training.	
"	25th "	"	The General Officer Commanding 3rd Cavalry Division inspected the Regiment and expressed his satisfaction with the efficiency and methods of training of the Regiment.	
"	26th "	"	Training.	
"	27th "	"	Training.	
"	28th "	"	Training.	
"	29th "	"	Training. Lieut.A.H.CLARKE, R.A.M.C., attached for duty.	
"	30th "	"	Regiment attended Divine Service. Capt E.A.Green proceeded to LE TOUQUET to attend a Course at the Hotchkiss Riffle School.	

Army Form C. 2118.

WAR DIARY
or
INTELLIGENCE SUMMARY.

(Erase heading not required.)

NORTH SOMERSET YEOMANRY 1st to 30th SEPTEMBER 1917

Instructions regarding War Diaries and Intelligence Summaries are contained in F. S. Regs., Part II. and the Staff Manual respectively. Title pages will be prepared in manuscript.

Place	Date	Hour	Summary of Events and Information	Remarks and references to Appendices
HAVERSKERQUE	30th September		2nd Lieut.W.H.ALLEN and 46 Other Ranks rejoined from XIII Corps. 2nd Lieut.N.RICHARDS proceeded to attend a Course at the 1st Army Sniping School, LINGHEM.	

Lieut.Colonel,
Commanding North-Somerset Yeomanry.

Vol 30

WAR DIARY

NORTH SOMERSET YEOMANRY.

1st to 31st October 1917.

VOL. No 36.

Army Form C. 2118.

WAR DIARY
or
INTELLIGENCE SUMMARY.

(Erase heading not required.)

NORTH SOMERSET YEOMANRY. 1st to 31st October 1917.

Instructions regarding War Diaries and Intelligence Summaries are contained in F. S. Regs., Part II. and the Staff Manual respectively. Title pages will be prepared in manuscript.

Place	Date	Hour	Summary of Events and Information	Remarks and references to Appendices
HAVERSKERQUE.	1st October.	In Billets.	Training. 2nd Lieut. F.W.LINDREA transferred to Special Reserve of Officers, Coldstream Guards, Struck off strength.	
do	2nd October.	do	Training. 30 N.C.Os & Men transferred to the Base.	
do	3rd do	do	Regiment held Regimental Sports.	
do	4th do	do	Regimental Scheme. 6 Remounts joined from the Base. The following Officers joined as reinforcements. 2nd Lieuts.H.L.SHAW, K.G.JENKINS, J.H.HEWES. 2nd Lieut.C.S.CAMPBELL rejoined from Hospital. 3/10/17.	
do	5th do	do	Regiment took part in Brigade Scheme.	
do	6th do	do	Saddlery and Kit Inspection. Lieut. G.BABINGTON proceeded to 6th Cavalry Brigade H.Q. to attend a Staff Course of 1 month.	
do	7th do	do	Regiment attended Divine Service.	
do	8th do	do	Lieut. E.A.HUTCHINGS evacuated to England (sick) 28/9/17.	
do	9th do	do	Training. Captain W.D.M.WILLS, North Somerset Yeomanry, Divisional Claims Officer, 3rd Cavalry Division, awarded the MERITE AGRICOLE.	
do	10th do	do	Training.	
do	11th do	do	Training.	
do	12th do	do	Training.	
do	13th do	do	Saddlery & Kit Inspections.	

Army Form C. 2118.

WAR DIARY or INTELLIGENCE SUMMARY.

(Erase heading not required.)

NORTH SOMERSET YEOMANRY.

Instructions regarding War Diaries and Intelligence Summaries are contained in F. S. Regs., Part II. and the Staff Manual respectively. Title pages will be prepared in manuscript.

Place	Date	Hour	Summary of Events and Information	Remarks and references to Appendices
HAVERSKERQUE	14th October.	In Billets.	Regiment attended Divine Service. 2nd Lieut. K.G. JENKINS promoted Lieutenant, with precedence as from June 1st 1916. (July 31st.) London Gazette 9/10/17. 2nd Lieut. O.M. DOBINGTON invalided to England, 6/10/17. Capt. E.A. GREEN rejoined from Hotchkiss School at LE TOUQUET.	
do	15th	do	Training. Lieut. B. BELLOT & 3 N.C.Os commenced a Course in the use of the Stokes Mortar at the 11th Corps School, MERVILLE 8 Remounts joined from the Base.	
do	16th	do	Training.	
do	17th	do	Training.	
do	18th	do	Training. 2nd Lieut. N. RIC HARDS rejoined from 1st Army Sniping School, LINGHEM, 17/10/17.	
do	19th	do	Regiment marched to a new billeting area at VALHUON-BRITEL and GROSSART. Regiment paraded at 7-30 a.m. and marched via BUSNES-LILLERS-PERNES.	
VALHUON	20th	do	Lieut B. BELLOT & 3 N.C.Os. rejoined from Stokes Mortar Class at 11th Corps School, MERVILLE.	
do	21st	do	Regiment attended Divine Service.	
do	22nd	do	Regiment marched with Brigade to new billets in the FREVENT area & paraded at 8-30 a.m. Regiment billeted at SIBBIVILLE-SERICOURT-FREVENT-GRAND BOUQET. March route ST POL - LEVEL CROSSING N.E. of FRAMECOURT.	
SERICOURT.	23rd	do	Regiment paraded at 7-30 a.m. & marched with Brigade to new billets at FIEFFES-BONNEVILLE-MONTRELET. Route, Main FREVENT-DOULLENS Road	

Army Form C. 2118.

WAR DIARY or INTELLIGENCE SUMMARY.

(Erase heading not required.)

NORTH SOMERSET YEOMANRY.

Instructions regarding War Diaries and Intelligence Summaries are contained in F. S. Regs., Part II. and the Staff Manual respectively. Title pages will be prepared in manuscript.

Place	Date	Hour	Summary of Events and Information	Remarks and references to Appendices
BONNEVILLE.	24th October.	in Billets.	to HTE VISE—HEM—FIENVILLERS.	
			Regiment paraded at 8-45 a.m. and marched to new Billets at LIMEUX- DUNCQ-LIERCOURT-BRAY-ERONDELLE-FONTAINE. Route, L'ETOILE-CONDE.	
LIMEUX,	25th	do	Stables	
			Improvements to Squadrons & Billets. Following Officers joined as reinforcements. 2nd Lieut. R.J.N.TAYLOR, 2nd Lieut. C.S.DOWDING, 2nd Lieut. R.B.BOWERMAN, 2nd Lieut. W.G.N.HAKEMAN, 2nd Lieut. A.S. HARLEY.	
do	26th	do	Improvements to Stables & Billets.	
do	27th	do	Improvements to Stables & Billets.	
			Lieuts. K.G.JENKINS and R.E.F.COURAGE, 98 Other Ranks proceeded by lorry to DOINGT as the N.S.Y.Detachment of the 6th Cavalry Brigade Co, 3rd Cavalry Division Pioneer Batt. London Gazette dated 23rd October 1917. Lieuts. to have pay & allowances of that rank (July 1st). K.G.JENKINS 2nd Lieuts. to be Lieuts. (July 1st) M.C.BIGGS, R.J.N.TAYLOR, W.B. STARKY, W.H.L.SHEPPARD, F. LUFF, V.C.RICE, M.C. (Aug. 23rd) C.S.CAMPBELL (Sept. 13th) R.E.F.COURAGE (Sept. 27th) E.A.HUTCHINGS, (Sept. 30th).	
do	28th	do	A & C. Squadrons attended Divine Service. Regimental Headquarters moved Billets from LIMEUX to EAUCOURT.	
EAUCOURT.	29th	do	Improvements to Stables & Billets. 2 horses joined from 6th Cavalry Brigade, 26/10/17 & 5 Chargers from Remount Depot, ABBEVILLE, 27/10/17.	
do	30th	do	Improvements to Stables and Billets.	

Army Form C. 2118.

WAR DIARY
or
INTELLIGENCE SUMMARY.

NORTH SOMERSET YEOMANRY.

(Erase heading not required.)

Instructions regarding War Diaries and Intelligence Summaries are contained in F. S. Regs., Part II. and the Staff Manual respectively. Title pages will be prepared in manuscript.

Place	Date	Hour	Summary of Events and Information	Remarks and references to Appendices
BAUCOURT.	31st October.		In Billets. Improvements to Stables & Billets.	
			[signature]	
			Lieut-Colonel,	
			Commanding North Somerset Yeomanry.	

A6945 Wt. W1422/M1160 350,000 12/16 D. D. & L. Forms/C./2118/14.

Vol 31

War Diary.

North Somerset Yeomanry.

1st to 30th November 1917

Vol. No. 37

WAR DIARY or INTELLIGENCE SUMMARY.

NORTH SOMERSET YEOMANRY.

Army Form C. 2118.

1st to 30th November 1917.

Place	Date	Hour	Summary of Events and Information	Remarks and references to Appendices
BAUCOURT.	1/11/17.	In Billets.	Training.	
do	2/11/17.	do	Training.	
do	3/11/17.	do	Training. 2 Men joined as reinforcements.	
do	4/11/17.	do	Regiment attended Divine Service. Major C.H.DRIMMIE (21st L.) proceeded to DAOURS as an Instructor at the 3rd Cavalry Division School. Captain E.NICHOLSON, A.V.C. joined and took over Veterinary charge of the Regiment.	
do	5/11/17.	do	Training. 2nd Lieut. A.S.HARLEY, Sgts. KEYES and RUSSELL and Cpl. WATTS. proceeded to ST POL to attend a course of instruction at the Physical & Bayonet Training School.	
do	6/11/17.	do	Training.	
do	7/11/17	do	Training. Captain E.A.GREEN proceed to LE TOUQUET as instructor at the Hotchkiss Rifle Branch of G.H.Q. S.A.School. Lieut. G.BABINGTON proceeded from 6th Cavalry Brigade to Cavalry Corps for attachment.	
do	8/11/17	do	Training.	
do	9/11/17.	do	The Horses of the Regiment were paraded at BROXDELLE at 9-45 a.m. for inspection by the Divisional Commander, but owing to rain the inspection was cancelled. 2nd Lieut. R.B.BOWERMAN proceeded to attend a course of instruction at the 3rd Army Signalling School, PAS.	
do	10/11/17.	do	Lieut. C.S.CAMPBELL admitted to Hospital on 10/11/17.	

NORTH SOMERSET YEOMANRY.

\- 2 - **WAR DIARY** or **INTELLIGENCE SUMMARY**.

(Erase heading not required.) 1st to 30th November 1917.

Army Form C. 2118.

Place	Date	Hour	Summary of Events and Information	Remarks and references to Appendices
BEAUCOURT.	11/11/17.	In Billets.		
do	12/11/17.	do	Training. 2nd Lieut. W.H.ALLEN proceeded to attend a course of instruction at the 3rd Army Musketry School, WARLOY BAILLON.	
do	13/11/17.	do	Training. Staff Ride under Commanding Officer for Squadron Leaders and 2nd in Command of Squadrons, and Signalling Officer.	
do	14/11/17.	do	Training. Major C.H.DELMEGE rejoined from 3rd Cavalry Divisional School of instruction. Lieut. R.E.F.COURAGE and 32 Other Ranks rejoined from 3rd Cavalry Division Pioneer Battalion.	
do	15/11/17.	do	Lieut. K.G.JENKINS and 52 Other Ranks rejoined from 3rd Cavalry Division Pioneer Battalion.	
do	16/11/17.	do	Training.	
do	17/11/17	do	6th Cavalry Brigade marched to new Billeting Area. (Ref. Map. 1/100,000 Sheets. ABBEVILLE and AMIENS.) Regiment paraded at FONTAINE Church at 8-45 a.m. and proceeded to Brigade rendezvous at FLIXECOURT at 10-30 a.m. March Route - VIGNACOURT - FLESSELLES - VILLERS BOCAGE - MOLLIENS au BOIS. Regiment billeted at BEHENCOURT and MONTIGNY.	
BEHENCOURT.	18/11/17.	do	6th Cavalry Brigade marched to new Area (Ref. Map. 1/100,000 Sheet AMIENS) Regiment paraded at 4 p.m. and proceeded to Brigade rendezvous N of BONNAY at 5-15 p.m. March Route - BONNAY - Road Junction 220 yards N of R. of CORBIE - Pt. 102 N of VAUX - BRAY sur SOMME. Regiment camped in huts at CAPPY.	
CAPPY.	19/11/17.	In Camp.	Orders received on evening of 19/11/17 that zero hour for the operations of the 3rd Army in the CAMBRAI Area was 6-20 a.m. 20/11/17 and Regiment orders were to be saddled up and ready to move by 8-30 a.m. on that date. Sgt. BOND proceeded to Hotchkiss Rifle School, LE TOUQUET.	

NORTH SOMERSET YEOMANRY. - 3 - **WAR DIARY** or **INTELLIGENCE SUMMARY**.   Army Form C. 2118.

Instructions regarding War Diaries and Intelligence Summaries are contained in F. S. Regs., Part II. and the Staff Manual respectively. Title pages will be prepared in manuscript.

(Erase heading not required.) 1st to 30th November 1917.

Place	Date	Hour	Summary of Events and Information	Remarks and references to Appendices
CAPPY.	20/11/17.		In Camp. Regiment saddled up ready to move at 8-30 a.m. Orders received that horses could be off saddled, but the Regiment to be ready to move at one hour's notice. Orders received at 8-45 a.m. that Regiment to be ready to move at half-hours notice from 6-30 a.m. 21/11/17. 2nd Lieut. N.RICHARDS admitted to Hospital.	
do	21/11/17.		do At 8-40 a.m. orders were received that horses may be off saddled, but Regiment to be ready to move at half-hours notice, after receipt of orders. At 4-15 p.m. orders were received that the Regiment would not move that night unless orders to the contrary are issued. Regiment to be saddled up, ready to leave Camp at 6-30 a.m. 22/11/17. 5-45 p.m. Regiment placed on 4 hours notice of readiness. 11-15 p.m. Regiment ordered to be ready to move at 1 hours notice.	
do	22/11/17.		do Regiment stood to at 1 hours notice until 3-30 p.m. when orders were received that 6th Cavalry Brigade were no longer required to stand to in a state of readiness.	
do	23/11/17.		do Regiment paraded at 8-30 a.m. & marched with Brigade to the CONTAY area. Route :- LE CARCAILLOT - MEAULTE - DERNACOURT - BUIRE - Road Junction 400 yards N. of RIBEMONT Church - BAIZIEUX - WARLOY BAILLON - CONTAY. (Ref. Map.1/100000 Sheets AMIENS and LENS). Regiment billeted at CONTAY.	
CONTAY.	24/11/17.		In Billets. 2 p.m. Orders received that 3rd Cavalry Division may possibly return to BRAY Area to-day. 8-45 p.m. Orders received to be in readiness to move at 1 hours notice from 7-30 a.m. 25/11/17.	
do	25/11/17.		do Regiment stood to at 1 hours notice until 8-45 p.m. when orders were received that the Brigade would not be in a state of readiness to move until further orders. 2nd Lieut A.S.HANLEY & 3 N.C.Os. rejoined on completion of course at Physical and Bayonet Training Base School, CAMIERS, POL.	

WAR DIARY or INTELLIGENCE SUMMARY

NORTH SOMERSET YEOMANRY.

1st to 30th November 1917.

Army Form C. 2118.

Place	Date	Hour	Summary of Events and Information	Remarks and references to Appendices
CONTAY.	26/11/17.	In Billets.		
do	27/11/17.	do	Major C.H. DELMEGE proceeded to the Divisional School at LAUCRS as an Instructor.	
do	28/11/17	do		
do	29/11/17	do	Lieut. W.H.L. SHEPPARD, 2nd Lieut. A.S. HARLEY, commenced a course of instruction at the 5th Army Sniping School at VADENCOURT.	
do	30/11/17.	do	Regiment ordered to be in readiness to move at one hours notice in Gap formation, or to furnish a Dismounted Company.	

Lieut-Colonel.,
Commanding North Somerset Yeomanry.

96/32

WAR DIARY.

NORTH SOMERSET YEOMANRY

1st. to 31st DECEMBER 1917.

Vol. No 38.

Army Form C. 2118.

WAR DIARY
or
INTELLIGENCE SUMMARY.

NORTH SOMERSET YEOMANRY

N. Somerset Yeo

(Erase heading not required.)   1st to 31st DECEMBER 1917

Instructions regarding War Diaries and Intelligence Summaries are contained in F. S. Regs., Part II. and the Staff Manual respectively. Title pages will be prepared in manuscript.

Place	Date	Hour	Summary of Events and Information	Remarks and references to Appendices
CONTAY	1/12/17	In Billets.	Capt.R.A.WEST, Capt.G.M.GIBBS, ~~Captain~~ Lieut.M.C.BIGGS, Lieut.F.LUFF, 2nd Lieut.J.H.HEWES, 2nd Lieut.C.PATES, and 196 O.R. proceeded with 6th Dismounted Brigade Battalion, to BERNES, for attachment to the 7th Corps. Lt. K.O.J.HAWKINS?	
	2/12/17	do.	165820 L/C SMITH proceeded to LIGNY St FLOCHEL to attend course of instruction in Stokes' Trench Mortars. Exercise and grooming. 4 remounts joined.	
	3/12/17.	do.	Exercise and grooming. L.3C.BALE I., L/C PARFITT F.G. and Pte KETTLETY A.S proceeded to DOULLENS for Stokes' Trench Mortar Course.	
	4/12/17	do.	Exercise and grooming. 2nd Lieut.W.F.ALLEN rejoined from 3rd Army Musketry School.	
	5/12/17	do.	Exercise and grooming.	
	6/12/17	do.	Exercise and grooming.	
	7/12/17	do	Exercise and grooming. Lieut.B.BELLOT, Lieut.H.L.SHAW and Lieut R.J.W TAYLOR proceeded to Divisional School, DACURS.	
	8/12/17	do.	Exercise and grooming. Capt.H.W.POPE, M.C. 7 D.G., and Sgt CURTIS W.J Pte BIGGS A H.G., Pte BARTLETT A.J., Pte POLLEN A., Pte GIBBS P.A., Pte MILLER C., and Pte WESTLAKE S.G. mentioned in Cavalry Corps Routine Order 556, for bravery in helping to extinguish a fire in billets at BROXELLE. Sgt BOND W.M. rejoined from Hotchkiss Course.	
	9/12/17	do|	Exercise and grooming. Capt. W.W.POPE M.C., 7 D.G. proceeded on leave to England from 19/12/17 to 24/12/17. 2nd Lieut.M.RICHARDS evacuated to England, sick, 28/11/17.	
	10/12/17.	do.	Exercise and grooming. C.S.M STOKES A.E. Army Gymnastic Staff attached to instruct in Physical and Bayonet Training.	

2353 Wt. W2544/1454 700,000 5/15 D.D.&L. A.D.S.S./Forms/C. 2118.

Army Form C. 2118.

WAR DIARY
or
INTELLIGENCE SUMMARY.
(Erase heading not required.)

NORTH SOMERSET YEOMANRY   1st to 31st DECEMBER 1917

Instructions regarding War Diaries and Intelligence
Summaries are contained in F. S. Regs., Part II.
and the Staff Manual respectively. Title pages
will be prepared in manuscript.

Place	Date	Hour	Summary of Events and Information	Remarks and references to Appendices
CONTAY	11/12/17	In billets	Exercise and grooming. Lieut. R.E.P.COURAGE and 2/O.R. proceeded to port of embarkation for 81 horses for uses in Egypt (as conducting party).	
	12/12/17	do.	Exercise and grooming. Armourer S.Sgt KEMP W.L. proceeded for duty to Divisional Armourer's Workshop, at CORBIE. Lieut.C.J.HANNAM proceeded to Cavalry Corps Equitation School at CAYEUX-sur-MER.	
	13/12/17	do.	Exercise and grooming. Cpl. MOODY F.G. reported wounded (accidentally) on 10th.	
	14/12/17	do.	Exercise and grooming.	
	15/12/17	do.	Exercise and grooming.	
	16/12/17	do.	Regiment attended Divine Service.	
	17/12/17	do.	Exercise and grooming. C.S.M.STOKES A.E., Army Gymnastic Staff rejoined 3rd Cavalry Division.	
	18/12/17	do.	Exercise and grooming.	
	19/12/17	do.	Exercise and grooming. L/C BALE I, and Pte KETTLETY A.S. rejoined from Trench Mortar course.	
	20/12/17	do.	Exercise and grooming.	
	21/12/17	do.	6th Cavalry Brigade moved to new billeting area. (LONGUET area) Regiment paraded at CONTAY Church at 9.a.m. and marched to Regimental billeting area LONG - L'ETOILE. Capt. A.H.CLARKE,R.A.M.C. Lt.Col.C.J.A.INC, D.S.O. 2 D.G., Capt A.W.PIPPS, Capt.&Adjt.T.A.PINN 18 H/ Lieut. W.H.L.SHEPPARD, 2nd Lieut. W.G.M.HAKEMAN, 2nd Lieut A.S.HARLEY, proceeded in relief to H.Q.Dismounted Battalion.	
LONG	22/12/17	do.	Exercise and grooming.	

Army Form C. 2118.

WAR DIARY
or
INTELLIGENCE SUMMARY.

(Erase heading not required.) NORTH SOMERSET YEOMANRY 1st to 31st DECEMBER 1917

Instructions regarding War Diaries and Intelligence Summaries are contained in F.S. Regs., Part II. and the Staff Manual respectively. Title pages will be prepared in manuscript.

Place	Date	Hour	Summary of Events and Information	Remarks and references to Appendices
LONG.	23/12/17	In billets	Exercise and grooming. Capt.C.H.GIBBS and Capt.R.A.WEST, 2nd Lieut J.H.HEWES, 2nd Lieut C.PATES, and 7 O.R. rejoined from 6th Dismounted Brigade. Lieut.R.J.N.TAYLOR, Lieut F.L.SHAW, and Lieut D.BELLOT rejoined from 3rd Cavalry Divisional School. Capt.A.B.MITCHELL proceeded on leave to PARIS 23/12/17 to 31/12/17.	
	24/12/17	do.	Exercise and grooming. 2nd Lieut R.B.BOWERMAN rejoined from 3rd Army Signalling School. Lieut R.E.F.COURAGE and 16 O.R. rejoined from port of embarkation of the horses of the regiment proceeding to Egypt.	
	25/12/17	do.	Exercise and grooming. Regiment attended Divine Service. 1 remount (Charger) joined.	
	26/12/17	do.	Exercise and grooming. Sgt HOWELL E.W. rejoined from the Base.	
	27/12/17	do.	Exercise and grooming. Lieut.F.LUFF rejoined from 6th Cavalry Battalion. 2nd Lieut W.H.ALLEN proceeded as Transport Officer to Dismounted Brigade. Lieut.W.E.STARKY and Cpl.SYMES F.S. proceeded to G.H.Q.,S.A.School. Hotchkiss Rifle branch to attend a course of instruction.	
	28/12/17	do.	Exercise and grooming.	
	29/12/17	do.	Exercise and grooming. 11 O.R. (Conducting Party of horses for Egypt) rejoined. Capt.H.W.POPE M.C. proceeded to Dismounted Battalion. Lieut.R.J.N.TAYLOR admitted to hospital.	
	30/12/17	do.	Regiment attended Divine Service.	
	31/12/17	do.	Exercise and grooming. 2nd Lieut.R.B.BOWERMAN, Cpl Mc INNES L.A. and Pte KILSBY L.J. proceeded to Cavalry Corps Signal School YZEUX to attend Power Buzzer course. Lieut.R.E.F.COURAGE proceeded 2nd Lieut.O.L.REE WILLIAMS to Tank Corps. Lieut.R.E.F.COURAGE proceeded in relief of 2nd Lieut W.H.ALLEN, Transport Officer, Dismounted Brigade.	

W.Lowry?, 2nd. Lieutenant,
Commanding North Somerset Yeomanry

Army Form C. 2118.

WAR DIARY
or
INTELLIGENCE SUMMARY.
(Erase heading not required.) 1st to 31st JANUARY 1918.

NORTH SOMERSET YEOMANRY.

Instructions regarding War Diaries and Intelligence Summaries are contained in F.S. Regs., Part II. and the Staff Manual respectively. Title pages will be prepared in manuscript.

Place	Date	Hour	Summary of Events and Information	Remarks and references to Appendices
LONG.	1/1/18.	In Billets.	Lieut. C.S.CAMPBELL rejoined from Hospital.	
"	2/1/18.	do	Capt. R.A.WEST & Lieut. K.G.JENKINS proceeded to Tank Corps, struck off strength. Lieut. B.BELLOT, 3 N.C.Os. & Men proceeded SALEUX for duty with Light Trench Mortar Battery.	
"	3/1/18.	do	2nd Lieut. W.H.ALLEN & 1 O.R. rejoined from Dismounted Division.	
"	4/1/18.	do	2nd Lieut. W.H.ALLEN proceeded to Tank Corps & struck off strength.	
"	5/1/18.	do	40 Remounts joined from the Base as reinforcements. Extract from London Gazette dated 4/12/17 & 7/12/17 respectively. "Major (Tempy.Lt-Col) William N.STEWART D.S.O. awarded Territorial Decoration". "Major (Acting Lieut-Colorel) G.H.A.ING, D.S.O. Dragoon Gds. mentioned in Despatches". Extract from London Gazette dated 1/12/17. "Lieut & Adjutant T.A.PINN, Hussars, granted the Acting Rank of Captain with pay & Allowances of Lieutenant whilst so employed 3rd August 1917." 2nd Lieut. R.B.BOWERMAN & 2 O.R. rejoined from attending Power Buzzer Course at Cavalry Corps Signalling School, YZEUX.	
"	6/1/18.	do		
"	7/1/18.	do	Capt. A.B.MITCHELL, Lieut. C.S.CAMPBELL & Lieut. H.L.SHAW & 5 O.R. proceeded to 6th Dismounted Brigade. 2nd Lieuts. C.PATES, C.S.DOWDING & R.B.BOWERMAN proceeded to BERNAVILLE to attend the second Course at the 3rd Cavalry Divisional School.	
"	8/1/18.	do	7 O.R. proceeded to join 6th Dismounted Brigade.	
"	9/1/18.	do	Lieut-Col. G.H.A.ING, D.S.O. rejoined Regiment having handed over command of the 6th Dismounted Brigade to Lieut-Col. A.BURT, D.S.O. 3rd Dragoon Gds. Capt. & Adjutant T.A.PINN, Lieut & Q.M. W.SHAKESPEARE, Capt. A.W.PHIPPS, Capt. A.H. CLARKE, R.A.M.C. & 6 O.R. rejoined Regiment from 6th Dismounted Brigade.	

Army. Form C. 2118.

WAR DIARY
or
INTELLIGENCE SUMMARY.

(Erase heading not required.) 1st to 31st JANUARY 1918.

NORTH SOMERSET YEOMANRY.

Instructions regarding War Diaries and Intelligence Summaries are contained in F.S. Regs., Part II. and the Staff Manual respectively. Title pages will be prepared in manuscript.

Place	Date	Hour	Summary of Events and Information	Remarks and references to Appendices
LONG.	10/1/18.		In Billets.	
"	11/1/18.		do	Lieut. W.B.STARKY & Cpl. H.S.SYMES, rejoined from attending a Course of instruction at the Hotchkiss Rifle School. LE TOUQUET.
"	12/1/18.		do	Cpl. McINNES L.A. proceeded to YZEUX to attend a 6 weeks Course of instruction at the Cavalry Corps Signal School.
"	13/1/18.		do	Regiment attended Divine Service. Capt. R.C.E.GIBBS took over Command of "B" Squadron.
"	14/1/18.		do	B. Squadron moved from L'ETOILE to new Billets at FONTAINE. No 165757 L/Cpl. BRINKWORTH C. proceeded to LE TOUQUET to attend a course of instruction at the Hotchkiss Rifle School.
"	15/1/18.		do	
"	16/1/18.		do	Lieut. M.C.BIGGS attached to 4th Brigade R.H.A. from 6th Dismounted Brigade R.H.A. from 21/12/17 as Signalling Officer. Capt. A.B.MITCHELL, Lieut.W.N.M.SHEPPARD, Lieut.C.S.CAMPBELL,Lieut. G.W.M.HEREMAN, 2/Lieut. A.S.MARLEY and 117 O.R. rejoined from 6th Dismounted Brigade. Capt. N.W.POPE, M.C., Lieut. H.L.SHAW and 73 O.R. remained in the Battle Zone as part of the 3rd Cavalry Pioneer Regiment.
"	17/1/18.		do	1 Reinforcement joined from the Base.
"	18/1/18.		do	Capt. G.M.GIBBS proceeded to Headquarters, Royal Flying Corps, for attachment as a Staff Learner.
"	19/1/18.		do	Capt. R.A.WEST, North Irish Horse, awarded Distinguished Service Order. (Extract. Suppl. L.G. dated 4/1/18.)
"	20/1/18.		do	Regiment attended Divine Service.
"	21/1/18.		do	
"	22/1/18.		do	Capt. A.B.MITCHELL proceeded to attend a Course at the 5th Army Infantry School, at TOUTENCOURT. No 165463 A/Sgt. L. WATTS M. proceeded to VADENCOURT to attend a Course at the 5th Army Sniping School.

WAR DIARY
or
INTELLIGENCE SUMMARY.

(Erase heading not required.) 1st to 31st JANUARY 1918.

Army Form C. 2118.

Instructions regarding ~~NORTH SOMERSET YEOMANRY~~ War Diaries and Intelligence Summaries are contained in F.S. Regs., Part II. and the Staff Manual respectively. Title pages will be prepared in manuscript.

Place	Date	Hour	Summary of Events and Information	Remarks and references to Appendices
LONG.	23/1/18.		In Billets.	
"	24/1/18.		do Lieut. C.J. HANNAN rejoined from attending a Course at the Cavalry Corps Equitation School at CAYEUX - Sur - MER. Lieut. W.B. STARKY & 71 O.R. proceeded as a relief of the North Somerset Yeomanry Detachment of the 3rd Cavalry Division Pioneer Regiment.	
"	25/1/18.		do Capt. H.W. POPE, M.C. & 64 O.R. rejoined from 3rd Cavalry Division Pioneer Regiment. 2 O.R. joined as Reinforcements from the Base.	
"	26/1/18.		do No 165163 Sgt. B.S. WILSON proceeded to ENGLAND to attend a Course at the Southern Command School of Musketry, HAYLING ISLAND.	
"	27/1/18.		do Regiment attended Divine Service. No 165756 L/Cpl. BRINKWORTH C. rejoined from attending a Course at the Hotchkiss Rifle School, LE TOUQUET.	
"	28/1/18.		do Brigade moved to New Billeting Area. Regiment billeted at PICQUIGNY. Regiment paraded at 11 a.m. & marched via CONDE - HANGEST.	
PICQUIGNY.	29/1/18.		do Brigade marched to Billets in the PROYART Area. The Regiment billeted at BAYONVILLERS and WEINCOURT. Regiment paraded at 8 a.m. & marched via ARGOEUVES - Road running N & E. of Citadel in AMIENS - DAOURS - I of FOUILLEY - WARFUSEE-ABENCOURT. No 165470 L/Cpl. HIBBARD R.J. proceeded to LE TOUQUET to attend a Course at the Hotchkiss Rifle School.	
" 3 BAYONVILLERS	30/1/18.		do The Brigade marched to the TERTRY & MONCHY le GACHE Area. The Regiment camped 500 yds N.E. of TERTRY (Ref. Map 1/40,000 Sheet 62C.Q.33.d.) Regiment paraded at 8-15 a.m. & marched on the main AMIENS - VILLERS-CARBONNEL Road, via FOUCAUCOURT - BRIE ↓ ESTREE-en-CHAUSSEE. On arrival in Camp the Officers, N.C.Os. & Men were accommodated in Nissen & Adrian Huts, Horses under temporary shelters.	

WAR DIARY
or
INTELLIGENCE SUMMARY.

NORTH SOMERSET YEOMANRY.

Army Form C. 2118.

Place	Date	Hour	Summary of Events and Information	Remarks and references to Appendices
TERTRY.	31/1/18.	In Camp.	2nd Lieut. A.W.HOLMES & 9 O.R. joined as reinforcements from the Base. Lieut. C.S.CAMPBELL proceeded on 30/1/18 to CAYEUX-sur-MER to attend a Course at the Cavalry Corps Equitation School.	

Lieut-Colonel.,
Commanding North Somerset Yeomanry.

Vol 34

WAR DIARY

NORTH SOMERSET YEOMANRY.

1st to 28th FEBRUARY 1918

Vol No 40

Army Form C. 2118.

WAR DIARY
INTELLIGENCE SUMMARY.

(Erase heading not required.) 1st to 28th FEBRUARY.

NORTH SOMERSET YEOMANRY.

Instructions regarding War Diaries and Intelligence Summaries are contained in F. S. Regs., Part II. and the Staff Manual respectively. Title pages will be prepared in manuscript.

Place	Date	Hour	Summary of Events and Information	Remarks and references to Appendices
TERTRY.	1/2/18.	In Camp.		
do	2/2/16.	do	2nd Lieut C.R.MASTERS joined from Base. Capt H.W.POPE M.C. and 30 O.R. working party on Green Line in CAULAINCOURT.	
do	3/2/18.	do	Regiment attended Divine Service. 2nd Lieuts C.PATES, C.S.DOWDING, and R.B.BOWERMAN, rejoined from 3rd Cavalry Divisional School. Working party on Green Line 1 Officer and 30 O.R. Capt. A.E.MITCHELL rejoined from attending a Course at the 5th Army Infantry School TOUTENCOURT.	
do	4/2/18.	do	Working party Green Line, 1 Officer and 30 O.R. Lieut M.C.BIGGS seconded to R.E. for duty with Army Signal Service. 165153 Sgt WILSON B.S. 165448 L/Cpl PERKINS W. 165120 L/Cpl HANCOCK W.C. awarded the BELGIAN CROIX DE GUERRE.	
do	5/2/18.	do	Working party on Green Line, 1 Officer and 30 O.R. 2nd Lieuts C.W.TURNER, and E.A.MAIN joined from the Base.	
do	6/2/18.	do	Working party Green Line, 1 Officer and 34 O.R. Working party JEANCOURT 1 Officer 61 O.R. Lieut H.L.HILL joined from NORTHANTS YEOMANRY on transfer. 2nd Lieut A.S.HARLEY appointed Regimental Intelligence Officer.	
do	7/2/18.	do	Working party Green Line, 1 Officer and 34 O.R. Working party JEANCOURT 1 Officer 61 O.R. Lieut H.L.HILL, 2nd Lieuts A.W.HOLMES, and C.R.MASTERS to 3rd Cavalry Divisional School.	
do	8/2/18.	do	Working party Green Line, 1 Officer and 34 O.R. Working party JEANCOURT 1 Officer 61 O.R. Lieuts W.B.STARKEY, and H.L.SHAW and 67 O.R. rejoined from 3rd Cavalry Division Pioneer Regiment.	
do	9/2/18.	do	Divisional Gas Officer lectures to the Regiment. Working party on Green Line Capt F.W.POPE M.C. 1 Subaltern, and 100 O.R. Working party JEANCOURT 1 Officer and 51 O.R.	

Army Form C. 2118.

WAR DIARY
INTELLIGENCE SUMMARY.
(Erase heading not required.) 1st to 28th February.

NORTH SOMERSET YEOMANRY.
Instructions regarding War Diaries and Intelligence Summaries are contained in F.S. Regs., Part II. and the Staff Manual respectively. Title pages will be prepared in manuscript.

Place	Date	Hour	Summary of Events and Information	Remarks and references to Appendices
TERTRY.	10/2/18	In Camp.	Working party on Green Line Capt H.W.POPE M.C. 1 Subaltern and 100 O.R. Working party JEANCOURT 1 Officer and 51 O.R.	
do	11/2/18	do	Working party on Green Line Capt H.W.POPE M.C. 1 Subaltern and 100 O.R. Working party JEANCOURT 1 Officer and 51 O.R. 165463 a/Sgt.WATTS M. rejoined from attending a Course at the 5th Army Sniping School VADENCOURT.	
do	12/2/18	do	Working party on Green Line Capt H.W.POPE M.C. 1 Subaltern and 100 O.R. Working party JEANCOURT 1 Officer and 51 O.R. Lieut R.J.N.TAYLOR rejoined Lieut M.FRIEND Lothian and Border Horse joined from Base. from Base.	
do	13/2/18	do	Working party on Green Line Capt H.W.POPE M.C. 1 Subaltern and 100 O.R. Working party JEANCOURT 1 Officer and 51 O.R. Lieut M.FRIEND and 2nd Lieut B.A.MAIN admitted to Hospital.	
do	14/2/18	do	Working party on Green Line Capt H.W. POPE M.C. 1 Subaltern and 100 O.R. Working party JEANCOURT 1 Officer and 51 O.R.	
do	15/2/18	do	Working party on Green Line Capt H.W.POPE M.C. 1 Subaltern and 100 O.R. Working party JEANCOURT 1 Officer and 51 O.R.	
do	16/2/18	do	Working party on Green Line Capt H.W.POPE M.C. 1 Subaltern and 100 O.R. Working party JEANCOURT 1 Officer and 51 O.R. 165745 L/Cpl HIBBARD A.J. rejoined from attending Hotchkiss Course at G.H.Q. S.A. School LE TOUQUET.	
do	17/2/18	do	Working party on Green Line Capt. H.W.POPE M.C. 1 Subaltern and 100 O.R. Working party JEANCOURT 1 Officer and 51 O.R. 2 O.R. joined from Base as reinforcements. 4 Bombs dropped in Camp by enemy aircraft, 1 man No 165805 Pte NICHOLLS E. slightly wounded, remained at duty, no other damage done.	
do	18/2/18	do	Working party on Green Line Capt H.W.POPE M.C. 1 Subaltern and 100 O.R. Working party JEANCOURT 1 Officer and 51 O.R.	

Army Form C. 2118.

NORTH SOMERSET YEOMANRY.

Instructions regarding War Diaries and Intelligence Summaries are contained in F.S. Regs., Part II. and the Staff Manual respectively. Title pages will be prepared in manuscript.

WAR DIARY
or
INTELLIGENCE SUMMARY.

(Erase heading not required.) 1st to 28th February.

Place	Date	Hour	Summary of Events and Information	Remarks and references to Appendices
TERTRY.	19/2/18.		In Camp. Working party on Green Line 2 Officers and 80 O.R. Working party JEANCOURT 1 Officer and 40 O.R. G.O.C. 5th Cavalry Brigade inspected the Camp at 11. a.m.	
do	20/2/18.		do Working party on Green Line 2 Officers and 80 O.R. Working party JEANCOURT 1 Officer and 40 O.R.	
do	21/2/18.		do Working party on Green Line 2 Officers and 80 O.R. "A" Working party 1 Officer and 40 O.R.	
do	22/2/18.		do Working party on Green Line 3 Officers and 123 O.R. 2 O.R. joined from Base as reinforcements.	
do	23/2/18.		do Working party on Green Line 3 Officers and 123 O.R. 1 Officer and 20 O.R. working party at aerodrome on FLEZ - GUIZANCOURT road. 2 O.R. joined as reinforcements.	
do	24/2/18		do Working party on Green Line 3 Officers and 123 O.R. 1 Officer and 20 O.R. working party at aerodrome on FLEZ - GUIZANCOURT road.	
do	25/2/18		do Working party on Green Line 2 Officers and 120 O.R. 1 Officer and 20 O.R. working party at aerodrome on FLEZ - GUIZANCOURT road. 2nd Lieut G.N.EVANS joined from the Base. Lieut R.J.N. TAYLOR and 165216 Sgt HIGGINS.J. to Course of Instruction at 5th Army Musketry Camp PONT REMY.	
do	26/2/18		do Working party on Green Line 2 Officers and 120 O.R. 1 Officer and 20 O.R. working party at aerodrome on FLEZ - GUIZANCOURT road. 165774 Pte HANCOCK S.R. rejoined from attending a Course of instruction at the 5th Army School of Cookery.	
do	27/2/18		do Working party on Green Line 2 Officers and 120 O.R. 1 Officer and 20 O.R. working party at aerodrome on FLEZ - GUIZANCOURT road.	
do	28/2/18		do Working party at Aerodrome on FLEZ - GUIZANCOURT road 1 Officer and 20 O.R. 165094 Sgt STOKES G.H. to England for Cavalry Commission. Lieut G.B.BABINGTON with 165551 Pte PRATT & 165074 Pte HYETT R.L. rejoined from Cav. Corps Headquarters.	

COMMANDING NORTH SOMERSET YEOMANRY

Cav Corps ZP
Vol 35

6 Bde 3 Cav Div

WAR DIARY

NORTH SOMERSET YEOMANRY

1st. to 31st March 1918

Vol No 41

Army Form C. 2118.

NORTH SOMERSET YEOMANRY. WAR DIARY or INTELLIGENCE SUMMARY.

(Erase heading not required.) 1st to 31st MARCH 1918

Place	Date	Hour	Summary of Events and Information	Remarks and references to Appendices
TERTRY	1/3/18	In Camp.	Lieut G Dalrymple rejoined from Car Corps H.S.	
do	2/3/18	do	Capt r/Major T.A.PINK 18th Hrs rejoined 18th Hrs for duty on demobilisation (Authy. A.G.D.A.Q./10/1/SK6(a) dated 22/2/18)	
do	2/3/18	do	Regiment attended Divine Service. 166090 Cpl AMESBURY W.H. transferred to attend course at Cav Corps Signal School YZEUX. H55.015 Cpl FRANCIS H. R.A.M.C. transferred to N.S.Y. under Army Order 204 of 1916, as Private 27/2/18. (Authy:- A.G. HoCR 8136/A dated 27/2/16). I.O.R. rejoined from Base.	
do	3/3/18	do	Training. Lieut F. Luff granted Special Leave to U.K. from 4/3/18 to 3/4/18. Lieut M.C. Hill 2nd Lieuts A.W. HOLMES and C.R. MASTERS rejoined from Div. Cav Div. School.	
do	4/3/18	do	Training. Reserved 2/Lt G.B. MOUNT died in Hospital 26/2/18 2nd Lieut. A.S. DOWDING transferred to 1st Battn SOMERSET L.I. on transfer (Authy. BA/2103/1116 (b) dated 27/4/18)	
do	5/3/18	do	Brigade MTB & at T.Square Retron	
do	6/3/18	do	Lieut Col C.M. TURNER rejoined from Corps Gas School. UNDERS CARBOCHEN Regiment S.A.A. & at T.Square Retron	

WAR DIARY or INTELLIGENCE SUMMARY

NORTH SOMERSET YEOMANRY

Army Form C. 2118.

(Erase heading not required.) 1st to 31st March 1918

Place	Date	Hour	Summary of Events and Information	Remarks and references to Appendices
ISMAILIA	1/3/18		Training Lieut M. FRIEND evacuated sick to INARAID 2/3/18	
			160703 Sgt NIXON B5 rejoined from Northern Command School of Musketry Zeitoun Haifa 1/3/18	
			165/30 Sgt DIMBYLE C5 tried by Gen Court Martial on charges of (1) Wsg for UK Army and Batton service stealing Goods the property of Comrades Finding Guilty sentenced 35 days F.P. No 1. Wsg for UK army and awarded sentence not being Guilty to Regt	
do	8/3/18	do	Digging in and Delousing up of Camp to Being trained joined Junior 8th Cav Bde	
do	9/3/18	do	Digging in and Delousing up of Camp Lieut G. BEBINGTON to 3rd Cavalry Division	
do	10/3/18	do	Lieut BREWER and 30 O.Rs rejoined from Cav Light Horse Bn Bttyg 5a Cavalry Divn Capt R.G.B. GIBBS Proceeded on leave to UK	
do	11/3/18	do	Digging in and Delousing up of Camp	
do	12/3/18	do	Major CADELMEGE rejoined from 3rd Cav Div School, 58 Horses and 6 Mules transferred to 2nd Cavalry Division	
do	13/3/18	do	Regimental transferred to 6th Cav Bde. 8th Cav Bde linked A.Q to Bde Hdqr Capt Hon R.P MC RUCCADEAU to Machine Gun Batton 21st Div. Capt to Mahatwar HLC attached Period 2 to 10th March. Lieut-Col G.H.H. IRISING D.S.O.	
			Transferred on leave to U.K. From 1st to 20th March 1918.	

Army Form C. 2118.

WAR DIARY
or
INTELLIGENCE SUMMARY.

(Erase heading not required.) 13th to 31st MARCH 1918.

NORTH SOMERSET YEOMANRY

Instructions regarding War Diaries and Intelligence Summaries are contained in F. S. Regs., Part II. and the Staff Manual respectively. Title pages will be prepared in manuscript.

Place	Date	Hour	Summary of Events and Information	Remarks and references to Appendices
BRIE	14/3/18	In Camp	271 Riding Horses transferred to 1st Cavalry Division 8th Cavalry Brigade. TRAINED horses most Building Areas on line Bethencourt Brie - One party under Capt. N.B. of the Reg. proceeded by train the most party marched via BUSIGNY and CAIRE - EBULNHOIR. 1 O.R. found on strength overseas. Capt A.H. PHIPPS posted to Corps A.R. Est. duty or attached to Corps Hist.	
HIRAINES	15/3/18	In Billets	Regiment commenced reconstitution of LONGPRE Group.	
do	16/3/18	do	Lieut. Col. G.H.A. TOR D.S.O. Graded 1 Month's leave on A.D.L.332 7 of 1916 from 16 Inst (Attd. Car Corps No.1 59/15 seen 9/3/18)	
do	17/3/18	do	Lieut. T.H. HEWES reported Resumed Duty (Attd. MS Car Corps No. DMS i21/1323)	
do	18/3/18	do	[entry re: Lieut P.R. BRIDGES...]	
do	19/3/18	do	Telegram received from Lt. Col. G.H.A. TOR D.S.O. that unit arrived Marseilles return on New Hospital ...	
do	20/3/18	do	Capt. P.B. PITCHER M. transferred on loan to R.A. from 20/3/18 to 3/4/18. Lieut. B. BENOIT taken over to Hospital.	
do	21/3/18	do	No.622 S.S.M. TUCKER R.W. transferred to ENGLAND for commission to special cadet school (N.B. Parling).	
do	22/3/18	do	11 Horses sent for Veterinary attendant. 8 horses transferred to Remount Com. Pte.	
do	27/3/18	do	Lieut. R.D.F. TAYLOR returned from 5th Army Mustery Corps. Pont Remy	
do			15 Horses proceeded to MARSEILLES for use in EGYPT.	

Army Form C. 2118.

WAR DIARY
or
INTELLIGENCE SUMMARY

NORTH SOMERSET YEOMANRY

(Erase heading not required.) 1st to 31st March 1918

Instructions regarding War Diaries and Intelligence Summaries are contained in F. S. Regs., Part II. and the Staff Manual respectively. Title pages will be prepared in manuscript.

Place	Date	Hour	Summary of Events and Information	Remarks and references to Appendices
AIRAINES	25/3/18	In Billets.	Regiment standing by in readiness to move at short notice. 2 wounded rats.	
do	26/3/18	do	Lieut R.H. Taylor proceeded to attend Lewis Gun Machinery course at P.B.T. School, St Pol.	
do	26/3/18	do	Regiment attached to 111 Corps obtained orders to march to ABBEVILLE via NEUFMOULIN	
do	26/3/18	do	Regiment marched and billeted in 7th Rsp Hussars movements. ABBEVILLE as Remount.	
do	27/3/18	do	Regiment moved to stand to. Regiment marched into billets at L'ÉTOILE	
L'ÉTOILE	27/3/18	do	Regiment moved to stand to in readiness to march at short notice.	
do	28/3/18	do	1655 Reg Sgr joined 25 ponies from Regimental Reserve to horse at short notice at Cavalry Depot.	
do	29/3/18	do	86 S'plus Riding Horses transferred to Reserve Regt. Regiment stood to in readiness to move at short notice.	
do	30/3/18	do	Regiment continued to stand in readiness to move at short notice. Lieut Col Oppler D.S.O. rejoined from leave.	
do	31/3/18	do	Regiment attended Divine Service. Regiment remained at stand to in readiness to move at short notice.	

Willcox Col. / Lieut Colonel
Commanding North Somerset Yeomanry

www.ingramcontent.com/pod-product-compliance
Lightning Source LLC
Chambersburg PA
CBHW081532160426

43191CB00011B/1741